KEYS TO GOVERNANCE

Also by Yılmaz Argüden
BOARDROOM SECRETS

KEYS TO GOVERNANCE

STRATEGIC LEADERSHIP FOR QUALITY OF LIFE

Yılmaz Argüden

Chairman, ARGE Consulting
Chairman, Rothschild–Turkiye

First published 2011 by
PALGRAVE MACMILLAN

Palgrave Macmillan in the UK is an imprint of Macmillan Publishers Limited, registered in England, company number 785998, of Houndmills, Basingstoke, Hampshire RG21 6XS.

Palgrave Macmillan in the US is a division of St Martin's Press LLC, 175 Fifth Avenue, New York, NY 10010.

Palgrave Macmillan is the global academic imprint of the above companies and has companies and representatives throughout the world.

Palgrave® and Macmillan® are registered trademarks in the United States, the United Kingdom, Europe and other countries.

ISBN 978–0–230–27814–1

This book is printed on paper suitable for recycling and made from fully managed and sustained forest sources. Logging, pulping and manufacturing processes are expected to conform to the environmental regulations of the country of origin.

A catalogue record for this book is available from the British Library.

A catalog record for this book is available from the Library of Congress.

10   9   8   7   6   5   4   3   2   1
20   19   18   17   16   15   14   13   12   11

Printed and bound in Great Britain by
CPI Antony Rowe, Chippenham and Eastbourne

Dedication

To all who have shared their love and knowledge with me...

And to all who have provided me an opportunity to help address new challenges...

Contents

Contents

Preface

Good governance is the key to sustainability of our organizations and success of humanity in improving quality of life for all citizens of the world. Governance is much more than a set of rules or regulations. **Governance is a culture and a climate** of consistency, responsibility, accountability, fairness, transparency, and effectiveness that is deployed throughout an institution. Good governance starts with the individual and is applicable in all types of organizations, starting from the family and extending throughout the community, company, non-governmental organizations (NGOs), governments at all levels, all the way to global institutions.

In this book I try to outline the keys to good governance. What is interesting is that these principles, despite different forms of application, are common regardless of the size, complexity, and jurisdiction of an organization. Furthermore, it requires an understanding of "regarding the others, as you regard yourself" to become relevant. This understanding transcends the individual's interests and requires considering not only interests of others with whom we currently share our planet, but also the interests of future generations. Good governance is the key to effective utilization of our limited resources and not only improves the quality of life, but also ensures sustainability of life on our planet.

Chapter 1 introduces the concept of governance and its relevance for improving the quality and sustainability of life on our planet. The second chapter focuses on how we can shape the future and sets the ground for why we need to change our attitudes and behaviors to achieve a sustainable and acceptable quality of life on our planet. As the most important transformation required for a better world involves reshaping the global institutions as well as achieving a new wisdom in accepting people who were deemed outsiders into the decision making processes, the third chapter focuses on global governance. Chapter 4 introduces some tools for good governance in the public sector. Chapter 5 analyzes the role of good governance at NGOs, both as a means of improving their own effectiveness, as well as their roles in transforming electoral democracy into participative democracy. Chapter 6 focuses on corporate governance to ensure sustainable value creation by corporations. Chapter 7 focuses on the individual in attitude as the culture of the individual citizen is the key to good governance at any institution. It concludes by providing a recommendation to improve global governance by initiating global education reform. The Conclusion is followed by the Appendix. This provides an example of shaping the future of a nation, namely Turkiye.[1]

However, each chapter is independent of each other and the interests of different readers may be focused on different issues such as global issues, NGOs, private, or public sectors. Therefore, each reader is able to delve into different chapters or skip some of the chapters as appropriate to need. Nevertheless, I suggest that the first two chapters that introduce the concept of governance and shaping the future be read first and Chapter 7 read last.

I could not have gained the understanding of governance that I wish to share through this book without the opportunity to work with hundreds of colleagues in many institutions across the globe, including think-tanks, academic institutions, international organizations such as the World Bank, the United Nations, the Turkish Government, numerous corporations and NGOs. I hold them in the highest esteem and thank each and every one of them for their invaluable contributions towards the development of my ideas on this subject matter. I would also like to thank the colleagues with whom I had the pleasure to serve on boards of numerous organizations. I am also grateful to my teachers throughout my academic life who have instilled the importance of sharing knowledge and to my colleagues at ARGE Consulting, especially Pınar Ilgaz, Burak Erşahin, and İlkay Gültaş who have helped enrich the ideas discussed here.

This book would not have been possible without the able support of Lale Göçmez, not only with her eloquent translation of some of my original Turkish work, but also with her help in shaping the material. I am grateful for her help. I also wish to thank my colleagues at ARGE Consulting; my daughter Gizem, a consultant at McKinsey; Cem Kozlu, former Chairman and CEO of Turkish Airlines; Ahmet Dördüncü, former CEO of Sabancı Holding; and Erkut Yücaoğlu, Chairman of the Advisory Council of Turkish Industrialists and Businessmen Association (TUSIAD) for their review of earlier drafts.

---

[1] I specifically utilize the formal name of the country, The Republic of Türkiye (Turkiye), as opposed to 'Turkey' throughout the book, as I support the movement to popularize the name Turkiye in the international arena.

I should like to extend my appreciation to Keith Povey for his excellent editorial help, Eleanor Davey Corrigan and Hannah Fox for their diligent work to get the book ready for publication, and Stephen Rutt, Global Publishing Director at Palgrave Macmillan, for his enduring support.

My son Ege deserves a sincere acknowledgement for inspiring the cover design.

Finally, I would like to express my appreciation to Jacques Attali, First President of the European Bank for Reconstruction and Development; Frank Brown, Dean of INSEAD; Muhtar Kent, Chairman and CEO of The Coca-Cola Company; John H. McArthur, Dean Emeritus of the Harvard Business School; Gerhard Schröder, Former Chancellor of the Federal Republic of Germany (1998–2005); Jim Thomson, President/CEO of the RAND Corporation; and Muhammad Yunus, Nobel Laureate, Social Entrepreneur, and Founder of Grameen Bank, for their review and comments on the book.

It is my sincere wish that this book will be useful in the development of good governance culture throughout the world and will contribute to the establishment of trustworthy relationships between all types of organizations and their stakeholders, thereby ensuring effective, sustainable, and equitable resource utilization to improve the quality of life throughout the world.

YILMAZ ARGÜDEN

About the Author

Dr Yılmaz Argüden is a leading strategist, advisor, and board member of major public and private institutions, as well as a number of non-governmental organizations (NGOs)s. He is the Chairman of ARGE Consulting, a leading management consulting firm in Turkiye. ARGE has been recognized at the European Parliament as one of the best three companies "shaping the future" with its commitment to corporate social responsibility and is the first Turkish signatory of the UN Global Compact.

He is also the Chairman of Rothschild investment bank in Turkiye; board member of many companies in numerous jurisdictions; an adjunct Professor of Strategy at the Bosphorus and Koç Universities, as well as the Turkish Military Academy; an author of numerous books and a columnist focusing on business and strategy issues. He is, in addition, the Turkish National Representative of the UN Global Compact.

He is a renowned governance expert and a member of the Private Sector Advisory Group of the Global Corporate Governance Forum, as well as being the Vice-Chairman of the Governance Committee of the Business and Industry Advisory Committee to the Organisation for Economic Co-operation and Development.

He has a PhD in policy analysis from the RAND Graduate School. He is also an Eisenhower, Fulbright, NATO, and Tubitak Fellow, and a recipient of numerous leadership, distinguished citizenship and career awards. He was selected as a Global Leader for Tomorrow by the World Economic Forum for his commitment to improving the state of the world.

www.arguden.net

CHAPTER 1

Introduction

The word governance comes from a Greek verb "kubernáo," which means steering and was first used by Plato in a metaphorical sense. It then passed on to Latin as "Gubernar" and many other languages.

Human beings form social groups to achieve certain goals collectively. Steering a socially connected group requires an institution with membership[1] and a definition of the jurisdiction for that institution. Regardless of whether a social group is a family, a tribe, a sports team, an NGO, a corporation, a city, a nation, or even the globe, its membership, call it citizenship, involves certain rights, responsibilities, and authority. Thus, one cannot talk about governance without referring to citizenship. As Aristotle states: "He who has the power to take part in the deliberative or judicial administration of any state is a citizen of that state. And speaking generally, a state is a body of citizens sufficing for the purposes of life."[2] This definition clearly identifies three elements required for citizenship: rights, responsibilities, and authority. The dualism of citizenship and governance, involves the power to make decisions for the institution (the state), or for its stakeholders (citizens). In short, governance defines three aspects of power: how it is acquired, how it is exercised, and how it is legitimized and controlled.

First and foremost, quality of governance has to be judged by the performance of the relevant institution. Therefore, the goal of the institution has to be clearly defined as a matter of priority. Then, steering toward that goal requires defining decision rights and processes, as well as establishing a feedback loop to verify and control performance.

Governance is how an institution is ruled; it is how the authority, responsibility, and controls are exercised in the institution. Governance is relevant to any institution, small or large; for profit or not; extending from a single family all the way to global institutions that have an impact on our lives. Hence, governance is relevant for humanity for quality of life now and for its sustainability in the future.

Human beings, individually or collectively, pursue happiness but face limited resources. While the definition of happiness may change according to different people, scarcity of resources is universal. The needs or desires of people are never satisfied. Furthermore, expectations always increase as the previous ones are met. This is the reason why humanity continuously strives for development.

As population and mobility increase, the world continues to get "smaller." Therefore, our mutual interdependence increases and everyone needs to be able to mobilize the resources and goodwill of others to achieve their goals. That can only be achieved through gaining their trust.

Whatever the goals or expectations of any individual or institution are, effective utilization of limited resources is the key to moving in the direction of attaining them. Improving quality of management improves quality of life. Therefore, improvement should be a continuous process. This in turn, requires a passion for learning, dedication to sharing, and an environment of trust. Building trust requires an attitude change from a single minded pursuit of selfish goals to "regarding others, as we regard ourselves."

As human beings cannot achieve their goals alone, they establish institutions for collective action. Sustainability of the performance of these institutions requires sustainability of their governance mechanisms, which in turn needs the trust of its citizens. Trusted governance mechanisms require a new understanding of human rights and democracy. Human rights are no longer conceived in the traditional sense, i.e., in a sense limited to civil and political rights such as the right not to be discriminated against on the basis of race, color, sex, language, religion, social class, or political opinion; freedom of speech, assembly, religion, entrepreneurship, freedom of press, and the like. Nor can democracy be limited any longer to exercising the right to vote for electing representatives.

The evolving understanding of human rights and democracy is the ability of people to contribute to and influence decisions that have an impact on shaping their future. Human rights and democracy in a rapidly changing world refers to the extent to which large masses of people have access to sources of knowledge and to means of communication. This is the prerequisite for people all over the world to have a say in their future and to take part in decision making processes that directly affect their lives. This is the modern content of democracy and human rights.

Today, individuals' urge to shape their future collectively is greater than ever. Their quest for new ways of governance is leading to fundamental changes whereby individuals, private, and public institutions try to harmonize their diverse interests through complicated interactive decision making processes. New governance mechanisms involve new, variable partnerships and networks whose rules of engagement are yet to be formalized.

Today, "governance" signifies a transformation from a type of relationship where a limited group of people have the ultimate authority to rule others to a set of relationships where mutual interaction takes place in order to make desirable choices for all stakeholders. It involves the mechanisms, processes, and institutions that individuals, corporations, groups, and societies utilize in joint decision-making and implementation, in expressing their interest and in fulfilling their obligations as well as in solving conflicts. In this context, governance points out to the nature of mutual interaction among social actors as well as between social actors and public administration, and it contains the meaning of "ruling together" with the aim of helping individuals realize their potential for improving the quality of their lives.

Thus, the essence of good governance is ensuring trustworthy relations between the institution and its stakeholders. Trust is the foundation of sustainable development. Good governance is the key to establish common expectations, to devise effective policies and processes in order to achieve desired performance levels in a sustainable fashion. Governance involves the rights and processes of decision making and exercising controls in an organization to achieve mutual goals. In short, governance is about performance.

Good governance is much more than just the structure, processes, and rules of decision making and controls. Good governance is a culture and a climate of **C**onsistency (predictability), **R**esponsibility, **A**ccountability, **F**airness, **T**ransparency, and **E**ffectiveness that is **D**eployed (subsidiarity[3]) throughout the organization (the "CRAFTED" principles of governance.)

In the new millennium, societies demonstrate and experience highly creative and efficient forms of governance and they learn lessons from them. In this context, a new type of citizenship consciousness emerges. This new citizenship consciousness symbolizes a new identity that acknowledges its own problems, demands higher standards but at the same time plays an active role in the formation and realization of these standards, that creates solutions from within and that forms the necessary structures for this purpose: in short, this new identity has a determination to shape its own future.

To establish these structures, consistency is necessary at a global scale. Global consistency requires a convergence on implementing common values in all aspects of life. The solution has to begin at the grassroots level: if transformation and change can be inspired at all levels of society, the process to shape the future begins. The role of those who do not take part in the process will be limited in a future shaped by others. Thus, for sustainability of our institutions we need to consider new ways of involving all stakeholders in governance mechanisms.

The basic element of any community or organization is the individual. Therefore, the domain of governance starts from the individual and extends all the way to all humanity – global governance. Good governance takes place at four levels in societal life: (1) Individual, (2) Corporate, (3) NGO, and (4) Public Sector, which in turn has three layers: (i) local, (ii) national, and (iii) global. At all these levels, if the stakeholders are driven by common values of having an open mind for continuous learning (**curiosity**); an open heart for sharing (**responsibility**); a quest for effective utilization of resources for **value creation**; and accountability, consistency, transparency, and fairness for **building trust,** then the fundamentals are in place for establishing the rules of engagement for good governance, paving the way for individuals to shape their own future.

This book argues that good governance is key to sustainable development of quality of life, the values and behaviors that drive good governance are similar for all types of institution, and if we are to shape our own future, we need to start from the individual and our education systems.

NOTES

1 Membership to an institution could be mandatory or voluntary, and at times exit may be restricted, e.g., trying to exit membership from the mafia may have serious ramifications for the individual.
2 Aristotle, *Politics*, Book III, Chapter One. (Translation by Benjamin Jowett.)
3 Utilizing both meanings of the word subsidiarity: (i) as a principle of social doctrine that all social bodies exist for the sake of the individual and therefore social institutions should not take over what individuals can do by themselves, and (ii) in political systems, the principle of devolving decisions to the lowest practical level, empowerment.

CHAPTER 2

Shaping the Future for a Sustainable Quality of Life

Quality is exceeding expectations.

'God helps those who help themselves.' (Benjamin Franklin)

Excessive energy consumption in some regions of the world can lead to floods in some other region due to global heating. A disease neglected because it is rooted far in Africa might become a dreadful epidemic in America. A terrorist organization backed for hitting other targets may, in time, turn the missiles on its supporter. Humiliation and isolation of those with unconventional beliefs and opinions can result in reactions that threaten global peace. The solution to such problems lies only in the solidarity of all mankind. Consequently, governance systems and attitudes must also gain a global dimension as daily life increasingly does so.

Today, protection of free trade and clean environment, fight against terrorism and international crime organizations, and issues such as celestial property rights require supra-national governance structures. As important powers and functions are transferred away from the nation-state through consensual delegation of sovereignty, governance is inescapably becoming multilevel, as can be observed from the case of the European Union. The currently developing key issue is the mechanisms required for the inclusion of the masses into these multilevel governance structures.

There are two main threats originating from the nature of the globalization–localization dualism and their potential for both integration and exclusion at the same time. The first of these threats is the ethnic, national, or religion based conflict that displays a tendency to spread, and in some cases turns into ethnic cleansing. Stopping that particular nightmare will doubtlessly be one of the top priorities of a new global governance structure committed to the vision of democracy and equality. In addition to this threat that tends to divide people with their geographic borders, common ancestry or religious beliefs, there is the danger of discriminating against people on the basis of their social positions.

In order to address the root causes of these issues, good governance is required at all our institutions, both at the local and the global level. Global governance has two prerequisites. First is the representation of non-governmental organizations in the international arena alongside the governments. The past half-century has witnessed the emergence of a vigorous global civil society. Today a multitude of institutions, voluntary organizations and networks covering women's groups, trade unions, co-operatives, neighborhood watch associations make an important contribution in many fields, both nationally and internationally. They offer knowledge, skills, enthusiasm, a non-bureaucratic approach, and grassroots perspectives. Excluding these from the international problem-solving processes and restricting representation only to governmental level reduces the opportunity to develop creative solutions to global issues.

If we are to be successful in including, rather than excluding, all communities into global governance structures, we have to improve our ability to manage diversity. The past experiences of mankind can meaningfully contribute to the refinement of diversity management. Take, for example, Turkiye,[1] the proud custodian of the land and the civilizations that flourished in Asia Minor for thousands of years. When we look at the history of the Ottoman and Anatolian civilizations what we see is great fluidity between religions and communities. As an example, the Seljuk Sultan Izzeddin Keykavus II, whose mother was a descendant of the Byzantine aristocracy, routinely organized in his palace theological discussions between Christian priests and Muslim religious leaders. This tradition, particularly highlighted in its Sufi variant, embodies a philosophy of great tolerance and accommodation. Poets and thinkers like Yunus Emre, Haci Bektas Veli, and Mevlana Celaleddin Rumi are inseparable parts of the cultural make-up of the inhabitants of Turkiye. We learn from the historical records that Mevlana Celaleddin, the Sufi religious leader, poet and thinker of the twelfth century, regularly visited the monasteries to exchange views with Christian and Jewish religious people. Prominent Christian clergymen came from Istanbul to discuss with him certain theological issues. It was Yunus Emre, the great Sufi poet and thinker of the thirteenth century, who preached in one of his

---

[1] I specifically utilize the formal name of the country, The Republic of Turkiye, as opposed to "Turkey," throughout the book as I support the movement to popularize the name Turkiye in the international arena.

poems: "Regard the other, as you regard yourself, this is the meaning of the four Holy Books, if there is any."

Just as in the new movement of alternative medicine where the old traditions of eastern cultures are providing the keys to healing the body and the mind as a whole, the new developments in management thinking can benefit from the traditions of old civilizations. For example, the Anatolian tradition of accommodation and tolerance is the reason why until late nineteenth century the Ottoman political order did not experience ethnic discrimination.

What marked the Seljuk and Ottoman experience in this field was a very specific definition of the "self" and the "other" and an associated administrative form of social organization considerably different from that in the Western world. In this form of organization, the so-called "Millet" (community) system, different communities enjoyed a high level of autonomy and empowerment. This system also allowed non-Muslims to be appointed to administrative positions that required a high level of political and financial trustworthiness.

In the nineteenth century the rise of race based nationalism in the West also echoed in the Ottoman territory. The course of events constituted a chain of reactions, which paved the way for great sufferings in all parts of the society. Nowhere in the world does history proceed along a straight line. Despite the inevitably irregular advance, the fundamental context of life in Anatolia was one of coexistence between different groups. In that sense Anatolia's legacy to the world is one of great diversity management full of rich experiences. These experiences have, therefore, the potential to make a significant contribution to the international process of furthering the progress towards better governance of the world.

If we are to have good governance in our institutions, if we are to shape our future for a more sustainable world, we need to understand that this involves much more than the mechanics of governance: rights, responsibilities, and authority vested in different people. It also involves having the **right attitudes** and **culture** in not just those who occupy leadership positions, but also all who participate in governance mechanisms. At its greatest expanse, it involves all the citizens of the globe. Shaping our future requires a particular approach, outlook, and attitude.

STEPS FOR SHAPING THE FUTURE

Use Imagination to Arrive at an Effective Vision

To envision the future is the first step in shaping the future. The questions to set us on the right path are: what it is about the future that is important to us, and what it is we are trying to achieve? In looking for the answers to these questions, we have to balance utilization of our resources not only to deal with today and its immediate problems, but also to deal with what matters to us tomorrow. Once we identify what is important, then we can start to envisage how we can achieve it.

The major step for formulating the vision is to expand our horizon, and to eliminate the borders in our minds. The more prepared we are mentally to achieve a broader horizon, the better equipped we will be to take the opportunity to shape our future. This is the key for individuals, corporations, institutions, and countries.

If we can identify today the extraordinary talent in a child to play the piano, then we can enable him/her to develop this talent to become a virtuoso in adulthood, this takes time and commitment that is more readily achieved when starting young. If we have the foresight today to identify the talent and to guide that child to take lessons, and to derive pleasure from playing and persistent practice, we have also impacted that child's future. Serena and Venus Williams have become world class tennis players not only due to their inherent abilities but also because of the vision of their father and his supportive efforts.

Similarly for corporations, the future of a corporation is determined by the kind of values that constitute the foundations, and the kind of investments that are made at the beginning. A major part of a company's cost structure is determined at the time the investment decisions are taken such as the location, technology, and target customer base. Therefore, the more goes into the thought and planning process, the more flexible and productive the investment is likely to be. The initial process will impact the values, the life cycle, the employment potential, and the customer satisfaction that a company will be able to achieve in the future.

Shaping the future is not predicting it, or putting forth a decision or definition for it, because the future is fraught with uncertainty. Given the multitude of factors that affect the future, it is not possible to control them all at once. However, it is possible to identify some of the variables in the overall matrix that can be controlled or impacted. What is important is to be able to take the first steps in the right direction.

Another critical step for arriving at the vision to shape the future is also a relatively easy one: to be able to imagine it. We should not under value "imagination." It was the first spark that led Albert Einstein to develop his theory of relativity that reshaped scientific thinking. There was certainly a deep accumulation of scientific expertise behind that first spark, but Einstein himself emphasized the importance of this first moment by stating that "imagination is more important than knowledge." The instinct of the human being is to be continuously on the lookout for the better, and to look beyond the horizon. What makes the human being the master of the universe is his ability to think and to strive to improve his universe, his environment, his society, his market, and himself.

To conjure up the future realistically, we must know our environment well. This means we have to have an understanding of ourselves, our team, our market, our society, available technology, and the world. In this way we can envisage how we will meet trends and needs, and this forms the basis of our "vision." Vision enables us to put forth ideas about how we can change our world, to challenge the status quo, and to add value by developing new vantage points.

It is important for the vision to be effective. It should be focused enough to guide decisions, and aspiring yet realistic enough to allow for taking initiative as needed, easy to communicate, and also realistic enough to excite those that will be impacted by it. Vision is holding the real world in one hand and reaching out to tomorrow's world with the other hand. Vision starts with what is at hand, but expands the borders in the mind to usher in new horizons. Sony adopted its vision as "making products that will enable Japanese products to be identified with high quality," at a time the opposite was true and Japanese products were deemed to be poor quality!

People that can set out an effective vision are those that can identify a real need, determine how and by whom the need can be satisfied; they know what questions to ask, benefit from the experience of others, and know how to focus. They have a good grasp of where they stand, and are constantly evaluating what resources they have to mobilize to reach their target, whether the resources at hand are sufficient, what solutions technology is offering, where the world is going, and whether the timing is right.

If the vision does not take into account the uncertainty of the future, then it will either remain a dream, or be very conservative and narrow in its reach. Good vision must set the correct targets, must realistically be achievable, yet be challenging. To strike the right balance and seek the answers to the right questions requires a depth of knowledge and a scientific analytic mind. If our purpose is to shape the future, to envisage what it will be like, we must feed our imagination with knowledge. To mobilize all elements of society to prepare for the future, from the individual up to government, the most important tool we have is knowledge.

At the beginning of the twentieth century, one of the great leaders of the time, Atatürk, set out with a difficult vision: to establish the Republic of Turkiye from the ashes of the Ottoman Empire and align the country with the modern world. However, he had substantial and realistic knowledge of the state of both Turkiye and the world at the time, enabling him to assess how far he could go. He commanded his army with the simple mission of defeating the occupying forces from the motherland, Anatolia. This was a tough but achievable goal. Furthermore, if successful, it would have given defendable boundaries to the new nation. He did not try to resurrect the Ottoman Empire. He knew that with the resources he had, such a vision would not only be impossible, it would be unrealistic and anachronistic in the world evolving after World War I. Instead, he read the needs of the people well and chose to reshape the country toward a goal that they could understand. He mobilized and inspired his nation to achieve his goal of aligning Turkiye with the modern world, on which path Turkiye still continues. Furthermore, despite being a military leader who had achieved all his credibility with military successes, as soon as he achieved his goal of establishing the new nation, he established the motto of "Peace at home, peace in the world," which still leads the diplomatic thought process of the country. The "zero problems with neighbors" policy of the current Minister of Foreign Affairs, Ahmet Davutoğlu, has its roots in this dictum. No wonder that at a secret ballot Turkiye had 80% of the votes from all the members of UN in its bid for a seat at the UN Security Council.

Set up the Right Team and Motivate it

Once the vision is defined based on a sound assessment of the environment and equipped with appropriate targets and strategy realizing it still requires mobilization of resources. The question of which resources, what kind of people, on what scale, and with what technology, must be carefully addressed. To achieve change, we require massive resources, not only our own, but also those of others. To use the resources of others requires collaboration of other people and institutions that will share our vision. For others to share our vision and be mobilized around it, the vision must have credibility. It must be easy to understand, and those that will contribute must be convinced of the benefits. Naturally the nature of this collaboration will be different depending on whether we are dealing with a small team, a company, an NGO, or a state entity.

Communicating the vision in a way that will be clearly and easily understood is essential. People cannot assimilate an ideal that they do not know, understand, or feel the need for. To mobilize people necessitates a clear explanation of the vision enabling them to share it. Mobilizing people for change equates to managing a massive team. To get results, the team has to be motivated for the change and has to accept the new game plan. The players will be successful to the extent that they can assimilate the change. History shows us that realizing a vision does not happen through a chain of command. Mental change happens not by commanding people, but by appealing to their minds and hearts.

Establish Coalitions for Change

No matter how good our qualifications are, we cannot lead the change process if we cannot enlist the support of the people around us. Collaboration and establishing the rules for such collaboration jointly is critical for mobilizing the people that represent the resources that we require for change. Credibility, trust, and good communication enable us to share our vision outside our own sphere, and to establish an efficient coalition for change. A coalition is formed where interests coincide, not where they collide, and is rendered productive by the leader that manages it.

Forming an efficient coalition will also prevent the dangers of groupthink that may result from remaining within the same circle. A strong coalition will expand the resources that can be mobilized. Forming a coalition between people with different interests from different backgrounds is not a simple matter. The leader of the coalition must reinforce behavior and initiative that supports the vision by advertising and rewarding such behavior within the coalition.

Inspire New Leaders

A good leader is a person that knows that change cannot be achieved by a single leader alone. To think so would be an effective way to kill the process. Within the organization and outside, there may be many leaders of change. To inspire them by giving them the opportunity to encourage creativity and initiative and to reward it will expand the circle of people assimilating the change. Empowerment develops leadership skills of the team. Winning the hearts and minds of people is the best way to mobilize resources effectively.

Believe in Your Own Vision

Mobilization of resources to achieve the vision requires credibility. To convince people, companies, institutions, and individuals within society, we must first demonstrate our own firm belief in our vision and earn their confidence. Without this confidence, it is very difficult to mobilize others and their resources. Therefore the firm belief in our own vision is a prerequisite to shaping the future. Actions speak louder than words in convincing others about the vision.

Use Communication as a Tool of Persuasion

Rallying the team and the environment around the vision falls on the leader for change. The leader has to communicate well with the people around him. Particularly in the early stages it is critical to keep those that believe in the change together. Another way to define leadership is the ability to persuade those that start out with you to accept their position as one of a minority. Those that want change will be few at the start. This is not easy, because by nature most people want to be part of the majority.

The leader of change has to use the power of communication to overcome this mentality and inspire confidence. To be able to use communication effectively, the vision must be defined as clearly, simply, and unambiguously as possible. When we look at the common attributes of successful institutions, we see that they have not only formulated a vision that is clear and transparent, but they have also communicated this vision in a format that is easy to understand by all stakeholders, and have thus achieved the consensus for change.

Success breeds success. Therefore, prioritizing small steps that can produce results and advertising the success of such steps enables the initial coalition to forge ahead. The legendary General Electric (GE) CEO Jack Welch started out with the vision of "creating the world's most competitive enterprise." He placed great emphasis on change and free flow of communication to reinvent the company. His ability to articulate his vision clearly and to communicate it to his people formed the foundation of his success. He personally attended training programs, and took part in the development and performance evaluation of his top 750 people. By inspiring, motivating, and empowering capable people, by rewarding success, and by spreading involvement within the company, he has taken GE to a new level and remained in management for 25 years as a successful CEO.

Lead by Example

Confidence and trust cannot only be gained by articulating the vision clearly. We must also stand behind our vision by our actions, and show the people we want to use our enthusiasm to take the steps toward our vision.

The leaders who have had the most impact on human lives are the prophets. They have impacted lives not only during their lifetime but beyond as well. The reason for this is the full confidence they have inspired about their own devotion to the values and beliefs they uphold. Spreading their vision was more important to them than their own lives. Similarly, all legendary commanders have put their lives on the line to inspire their armies and led the charge. Congruity of word and deed is critical to demonstrating commitment to a vision.

Identify the Right Inflection Points

Another important aspect of shaping the future is identifying those critical turning points that we can impact. Since the future carries a lot of uncertainty and unknowns, it is not possible to control all the elements and make all the changes that we want to make. However, we should not undermine the small steps that we can take and remember that they can trigger larger changes. It is not easy to change the course of a large transatlantic ship in one single move or with force. However, by manipulating the angle of the propeller we can change the course of the massive ship by small adjustments. In order to do this we must know when to intervene to take it in the direction that we want. That is to say, if we have identified the correct time and place, if we make the change early enough and at the right point on the course, we can make a big impact with small changes.

Overcome Uncertainty by Confidence

One of the common attributes of big visionaries is their high self-confidence. It is not easy to overcome uncertainties without self-confidence, which is not to be confused with presumed self-importance of being able to do everything, and on one's own. Self-confidence is correctly identifying future risks and establishing the set up to turn change into an opportunity.

Inspire Others with Confidence

Self-confidence is the basis of the creative spirit and prowess that change leaders need. Leaders with self-confidence are not afraid to aim high. They then focus on their difficult targets, and in doing so take the biggest step toward reaching it. The leader that is shaping the future is on the one hand a person with a high level of self-confidence, and on the other hand one that has confidence in this team. Self-confidence enables the leader to overcome the challenges to reach his target and embolden the people around him. People with self-confidence are not threatened by the success of others but are supportive of it. Since the purpose is for everybody to reach the same target, the success of others does not foster envy within the group, on the contrary, such success is applauded and rewarded.

Leaders with self-confidence also admit they can make mistakes, learn from them, and change course as a result, if and when necessary.

It is important however not to be indecisive. A leader is someone that knows indecision can be more harmful than a wrong decision.

Manage Uncertainty and Risk

Since the future carries a lot of uncertainty, it is unavoidable to be faced with risks in implementing the steps toward our vision. Leaders for change must constantly keep sight of their vision to envisage potential risks. Just as they are not afraid to take on the initiative, leaders are not afraid to take on responsibility. It is not possible to shape the future without taking on risks. Taking responsibility and taking risks go hand in hand. Responsibility for foreseeable or unforeseeable risks rests with the leader. Taking risks entails making wrong moves every so often. This is where self-confidence comes into play.

We must see risks due to uncertainties as a part of long-term undertakings and brace them as such. The reason we want to shape and prepare for our future is in fact to manage the risks that drain our energy, narrow our horizon, and otherwise take our future hostage. We must regard risks as opportunities that will take the process of shaping the future forward, and should not let them endanger the process. If we adopt modern methods of managing risks, we can develop ways of overcoming them.

NORMS NOT SUPPORTED BY VALUES ARE INEFFECTIVE

Management style has a direct impact on how successfully the leader's sphere of influence can be prepared for change. The most result oriented and effective management style is one that emphasizes values. Establishing rules is not an effective way of management on its own.

This seems to be a common problem particularly in the state bureaucracy of numerous countries. Whenever there is an improper use of authority or of funds, a string of measures are implemented to prevent it from happening again. Over time such measures accumulate to the extent that they start conflicting with one another. Managing bureaucracy based on rules alone eliminates any use of initiative. People that live and work by rules alone cannot take any initiative. When there is no initiative, it is not possible to give quality service to meet the needs of constituents. This leads to procrastination in service. Moreover, since there are only penalties in case of failure and no rewards for good service, there is in fact no incentive to do the work at all. A pedantic management style prevents any initiative taking, atrophies creativity, and generally promotes "not working."

The reason for this phenomenon particularly in the public sector cannot be the employees. These people are not necessarily less qualified than those that work for the private sector. The problem is the system that leads to atrophy of its employees. Even going beyond developing countries, we see many examples of inefficiencies and lack of productivity that result from excessive bureaucracy of the European Union.

Another reason for the flaws of the state sector is favoritism. Generally the result of political populism, this practice ignores sound management principles, and appointments are made on the basis not of competency, but of loyalty. Many institutions and family companies fail due to this "illness" of failing to uphold meritocracy.

In order to prevent such congestion in the system, we must shift to managing by values rather than managing by rules. This was another tenet of Jack Welch's management principles, to the point that he said he would fire those that do not uphold the company values even if they delivered the results, on the other hand he would give a second chance to those that did not deliver the results, yet upheld the company values.

MANAGING BY VALUES: CONSISTENCY OF THOUGHT-DISCOURSE-DEED-OUTCOME

Why should we manage by values? Managing by values is the formulation of a whole between our values, our thoughts, our articulation of them, and our actions. In this management style, values shape the thinking, thinking shapes the words, words shape the actions, and actions shape the end result. The chain forms a whole. However in pedantic management, the rules guide the actions and rarely the discourse. People that do not understand the meaning of the rules and internalize the values that these rules were based on cannot implement or make the necessary adjustments when needed.

Managing by values enables the basic elements necessary to shape the future to come together. This kind of leadership increases levels of confidence and motivation, thereby increasing the quality of decisions and actions. In an environment of higher confidence and motivation, people trust each other more, and are not afraid to use initiative or take risk.

The most tangible outcome of leading by values is that it is result oriented and sustainable. When this leadership style is adopted, in the business world the customer, and in the state sector the citizen becomes the focal point. Therefore, in all actions and decisions, serving the people in our focal point becomes the pivotal norm. In a society where managing by values prevails, those that want to shape the future can gather around a common goal. They respect each other more, promoting an atmosphere of higher effectiveness and innovative entrepreneurship in all aspects of their life.

QUALITY OF MANAGEMENT IS KEY TO EFFECTIVENESS IN SOCIAL ENTREPRENEURSHIP

Effectiveness and innovative entrepreneurship used to be concepts that pertained only to business life. Now we use such concepts for every type of institutions and organization. Non-profit, non-government organizations (NGOs) are particularly prominent among such organizations. NGO entrepreneurship is playing a more and more important role in shaping the future in the twenty-first century. Social scientists champion this century as the NGO century. Appraising entrepreneurship only as a commercial concept and not placing a social value on it would be to ignore an important feature of shaping the future. For a wholesome approach to shaping our future, we must go beyond changing our public and private sectors. We must also change our societal behavior.

For example, in the areas of education, environment, and health, there are limits to what the public or private sector can do. However, if NGOs are also active in these areas, it may be possible to mobilize otherwise idle resources.

In Turkiye, the National Quality Movement (NQM) is an example of social entrepreneurship that has been instrumental in creating role models in different sectors and areas, and on different scales. NQM has been instrumental in developing a cadre of people who are not only the ambassadors of this philosophy, but also help numerous institutions develop their management systems professionally.

The National Quality Movement has its origins on the premise that Total Quality Management (TQM) is necessary not only to increase the competitive power of commercial enterprises but also to increase the quality of life for society as a whole. Therefore, TQM is no longer solely considered a management technique to increase commercial productiveness and competitiveness, but is gaining popularity among public enterprises, local administrations, hospitals, and NGOs as a philosophy of life to improve life quality.

NQM instigated significant achievements: evolution of management styles and investment into knowledge, skill, and experience resulted in major gains. Successful cases of TQM went beyond borders and Turkish institutions started receiving numerous international awards. The fact that Turkiye holds one of the largest number of European Quality Awards (European Foundation for Quality Management, EFQM) is proof that the success of these cases was not a coincidence.

NQM chose to promote implementation of the EFQM's Excellence Model to improve management quality throughout Turkiye. NQM successfully showed that TQM can be implemented in all areas, and the biggest gain was the implementation examples in the public sector, which traditionally held old and very established ways and was the least expected to adopt TQM. The Ministry of Education was the first to sign the Letter of Goodwill of NQM, providing the first example of a huge state sector actor, the Ministry of Education, supporting an NGO movement. Several other state entities or administrations including the Ministry of Labor, Turkish Military Forces, local administrations, universities, and hospitals have since adopted TQM, forming the basis for state reform, and demonstrating the contributions of NQM to Turkiye. NQM is thus gaining credibility in Turkish society by showing how a civil movement can work to improve "quality of life by quality of management."

NGOs SHOULD ALSO ACHIEVE QUALITY IN MANAGEMENT

Principles for successfully managing NGOs are not much different from those for a private or public corporation, perhaps even more difficult. As potentially successful agents of change in societal behavior, in order to be effective, NGOs should also adopt a participative approach to formulating and promoting their mission and vision; should be able to share these widely, adhere to good governance principles and show that they value transparency and accountability. Management of an NGO is however more difficult than management of a company, since the people that NGO managers are trying to direct are comprised of volunteers who are rather more difficult to motivate continuously. One of the basic conditions for success in NGO management is the credibility of the NGO leader in his support of the values he promotes. Social entrepreneurship requires close cooperation and communication with other segments of society. If we fail to prioritize communication for lack of funds, we are losing our ability to motivate and draw people to our cause.

When we define one of the basic functions of an NGO as helping reshape the stereotyped thinking patterns of society, we can see that developing content is as important as how well we communicate it. Impacting thinking processes requires well thought out substance.

Empty talk or easy solutions lack credibility. Real solutions are possible only if they are based on knowledge and research, and are developed by multifaceted thinking and emphasis on content.

COMPANIES RELY ON COMPETITION, NGOs RELY ON COOPERATION

It is more important for NGOs to develop cooperation and coalition by persuasion and communication than it is for private companies. This is because the NGO sector has very limited resources that they command and have unpredictable flow of funds. By definition companies have to be competitive in their chosen fields of operation. However, in the case of NGOs "cooperation" becomes the basic tenet of operation as opposed to "competition." Rather than compete for very limited resources, NGOs have to look for ways to increase resources by cooperation.

In social entrepreneurship, getting results is more important than who gets the results. The process of institution building is as, if not more, critical to NGOs, since it is linked directly to their reasons for existence. We cannot expect an NGO to have an impact on societal behavior if it does not display adherence to good governance principles itself.

COMMON PRINCIPLES OF SHAPING THE FUTURE

Principles of shaping the future apply equally in all segments of society. First, those who wish to shape the future have to have a dream about the future and develop thoughts and content for the desired future. Real results are achieved not by solving problems, but by catching the opportunities – "Luck favors the prepared mind." This is the essence of shaping the future. Shaping the future is preparing the mind, the behavior, and the attitude.

Second, the desired future has to create a value. Value-creating activities that utilize resources effectively tend to have a higher success rate. Innovation is the engine of development and value creation. Therefore, shaping the future requires innovative thinking and vision.

Third, those who wish to shape the future have to have a realistic assessment of the resource needs and how to gain access to them. In particular, one has to realize that resources are not solely, or even mainly, within the organization but rather outside the organization. Therefore, an open mind for cooperation, a commitment to meritocracy, development of the best, and fairness in sharing are the keys to mobilization of adequate resources. Those who focus only within the organization, as it is the familiar territory, are likely to have a limited vision and will be unable to achieve a broad acceptance of the vision and mobilization of resources.

Fourth, shaping the future requires a broad understanding of the environment, which in turn can only be achieved by those who have a passion for learning and continuous improvement. Those who are keen observers of the world, of the technological developments, of the resources, and their team are more likely to identify the important steps needed to shape the future.

Fifth, shaping the future requires creating trust and effective communication of the vision in order to win the hearts and minds of the decision makers regarding the required resources and those who are subjects of the change initiative.

Sixth, we have to realize that shaping the future starts with changing our own current behavior. Achieving a consistency in thought, values, and behavior is the best way to gain trust. Assuming responsibility for the future and utilizing all the resources solely for the stated vision is the most reliable way of mobilizing others' resources.

Last, but not least, shaping the future requires a long-term focus and discipline. It requires practicing for a marathon, not for a 100m sprint. Positive attitude and living a balanced life increases longevity and strength to realize the vision.

So regardless of which role(s) we hold in society, as long as we adhere to certain common principles, and as long as we are consistent in our thoughts and actions, we could be not only in a position to fulfill our responsibilities as a citizen of our globe, but also have the potential to influence the shape of our common future. Luck favors the prepared mind –it is the prepared mind that recognizes the opportunities and benefits from them.

Hence, those who will be able to seize the opportunities to shape our future will be those who understand the relevance of governance in all our institutions and act consistently to ensure that principles of good governance are adhered to.

Man lives by his dreams. It is of course important to have meaningful dreams. If we start today, we can pave the way to our dreams for a better future.

Look, the job of a leader and his or her team is to deliver to commitments in the short term while investing in the long-term health of the business. Bottom line: that's management. Good managers know how to eat today and dream about tomorrow at the same time. Any fool can just deliver in the short term by squeezing, squeezing,

squeezing. Similarly, just about anyone can lie back and dream, say-ing, "Come see me in several years, I'm working on our long-term strategy." Neither one of these approaches will deliver sustained shareholder value. You have to do both. (Jack Welch elaborating shareholder value, *BusinessWeek*, March 16, 2009.)

The same idea holds for any institution, regardless of whether it is for profit or not.

CHAPTER 3

Global Governance for Global Issues

Thought is the foundation of action.

'Every obstacle yields to stern resolve.' (Leonardo da Vinci).

GLOBAL CRISES TO GLOBAL GOVERNANCE

The mortgage crisis that started in the United States has had a more drastic effect on the citizens of countries throughout the world than the fall of the Berlin Wall or the World Trade Center buildings on September 11, 2001.

Remembering that the 1929 economic crisis was a root cause of World War II, one can easily appreciate that this crisis deserves our attention for reasons far beyond the economic ramifications of the current global crisis.

Beyond sharpening the awareness of Americans to the limitations of unilateralism, the crisis has also shown the Russians the fragility of depending on the ever-increasing commodities of oil and gas prices to finance the new rising of Russia. It has also demonstrated the dependence of the "Chinese miracle" on continued global economic growth – and the level of profound integration of economies across the Atlantic.

Contagion of this economic crisis seems to be much broader and faster than the SARS crises that started a decade ago in China and led to the quarantine of Toronto in Canada.

All of these events have a direct impact on our global governance systems. Attitudes should also gain a global dimension as our daily life increasingly does so. If a management guru coming from a different planet were consulted on how to establish a well-working governance system for the world, he/she would certainly not propose the current global structure. The fact that jurisdictions for key governance issues such as elections, taxation, military organizations are based on national boundaries set by people makes it difficult to organize on a global scale. Just as it would be almost impossible to run a factory optimally by asking the operator of each unit to run their machines optimally, the current organizational structure of the globe makes it difficult to agree on global priorities.

In thinking about global governance mechanisms, one could possibly learn from human institutions with longevity. While there are differences among the main religions throughout the world, religions have generally survived for much longer periods than even the mightiest empires. One of the reasons for this is that religions focus on basic principles whose aim is the sustainability of communities.

One of the common principles of religions is caring for and helping others who are in need (e.g., concept of almsgiving). Another is to have a perspective longer than one's own lifetime (e.g., concepts of hell and heaven or reincarnation.) As the world gets smaller and more interconnected, we have to understand that sustainability requires a perspective longer than an individual's life and that others' problems are also our own. If we fail to understand this, we will be endangering our own future.

For example, many religions ask for almsgiving to the needy. If we take our global responsibilities seriously, we should organize our global institutions in such a way that the rich countries contribute significantly to ensure that the global institutions have the means to deal with the problems of the poor. In a way, national almsgiving by the developed countries to the poor countries may be a more effective way of ensuring global sustainability than ever increasing defense budgets.

Common teaching of religions is that sharing with others builds more sustainable communities. Now with increasing global interdependencies, we need to understand that we live in a global community. As the world gets smaller and more interconnected, we have to attack the global problems jointly and apply good governance principles not only to our own governments, but also to global institutions.

Global institutions will gain real legitimacy only if people have a say about shaping their own future, to contribute in the global decision-making process. The content of modern age human rights and democracy is this. If we are successful in bringing democratic principles to the solution of global issues with the inclusion of all the interested parties in global decision making, we will be helping to achieve a more sustainable and secure world.

CONSENSUAL DELEGATION OF SOVEREIGNTY

The ongoing global financial and economic crises have made it clear that many of the issues impacting on quality of life throughout the world are global in nature. On the other hand, the way that humanity has organized itself, particularly on the public administration front, is national in nature. The fact that jurisdictions for key governance issues – such as elections, education systems, taxation, and military organizations – are based on national boundaries makes it difficult to organize on a global scale. Furthermore, as most democratic governments are elected for four- to five-year terms, the average perspective of an elected national leader is about two-and-a-half years!

It would be naïve to suggest dismantling national structures and moving towards a global government. Yet, longer perspectives and more collaboration are definitely needed to address global issues. Forward-looking politicians need the support of the public in such a collaborative approach. There is a need to create global institutions with adequate resources and decision-making powers that are shared and exercised equitably. For example, it is difficult to justify the lack of veto power for India at the United Nations when France has one, regardless of which objective criteria is utilized: number of citizens, economic might, or being a nuclear power. The current system is a relic of history that needs to be adapted to twenty-first century realities.

Yet, rather than lament past injustices, we ought to focus on the one positive aspect of the current situation, bleak though it may be: the fact of the matter is that crises sharpen minds.

National leaders just about everywhere – from India and China to Brazil and the United States – are coming to grips with the fact that global problems require global solutions. Global solutions can only be implemented with global cooperation. There is also much to be learned from other global experiences. As an example, Turkiye is a key G20 member and one of the three OECD countries that did not have to throw public funds to its banking industry during this crisis. Turkiye's experience during the financial crisis has been held up as a shining example – even by the United States.

Turkiye's success is due to the fact that difficulty bears capability. After Turkiye's homemade financial crisis of 2001 (which stemmed from a lax regulatory environment), the government instituted new independent regulatory agencies and stress-testing capabilities. These are now being studied by such institutions as the US Federal Deposit Insurance Corporation.

Global solutions require consensual delegation of sovereignty, in certain areas, to global institutions with adequate resources. Raising adequate resources for global institutions, in turn, needs appropriate power-sharing arrangements.

The Pittsburgh G20 meeting and the 2009 World Bank-IMF meetings in Istanbul pointed to a serious effort to strengthen global institutions in meaningful ways. Many ideas that were previously deemed marginal are now receiving interest. The G7, at long last, is being replaced by the G20 as the primary platform of global decision-making.

Another such example is the change in the voting rights at the IMF in favor of new emerging economies. For instance, China, South Korea, Mexico, and Turkiye have been beneficiaries of the changes in IMF voting rights. NGOs are also becoming a sounding board for these global institutions.

However, some are questioning if the adjustments are significant enough to create real change. There are still major steps to be taken to balance gross inequalities and bring more diversity and balance to the head table. Longer perspectives and increased collaboration are definitely needed to address global issues.

Unless the governance of global institutions such as the UN, World Bank, IMF, and NATO becomes more inclusive and balanced, it will be extremely difficult to increase their legitimacy and resources to match the problems they must now address.

The essential principle driving modern human rights and democracy is this: People should have a say in shaping their own future and be able to contribute in the global decision-making processes that influence their lives. **Global institutions will gain real legitimacy only if this understanding is applied to global governance mechanisms.**

In order to understand how global governance can be improved let us first consider two important pillars of democracy: the European Union and the United States and how the attitudes held by these two globally important organizations have the potential to influence global governance. Then we will discuss a global institution in need of change: NATO and finally a global issue that requires considerable care: the use of water.

GLOBAL EUROPE: EUROPE HAS THE POTENTIAL TO BE A ROLE MODEL FOR GLOBAL LEADERSHIP

For decades European development has been guided by a number of key values: human rights, democracy, and freedom of thought and belief (and of the press), free trade, the rule of law, laicism (in most countries), and multiculturalism.

Generations have been raised in an environment promoting these values. These values have been central to helping Europe achieve historically unprecedented prosperity and stability. Yet Europe now faces a number of serious risks for the future: an ageing population, eroding competitiveness, limited military credibility, and limited access to key natural resources. Global institutions seem inadequate to the range of global risks facing the world, from terrorism to climate change. The true test of values is whether they can be maintained when they run counter to short-term interests of these risks and challenges.

Some conflict is already emerging. Some key European values – such as free trade – are beginning to hurt. Globalization has the potential to make some people in Europe relatively poorer, even if it helps global growth. Will Europe continue to open its markets, and enable cross-national mergers, regardless of the nationality of new owners?

A similar question applies to transforming global institutions along Universalist lines, which may run counter to Europe's interests. For example, it is difficult to defend Europe's two vetoes in the UN Security Council when India has none. Will Europe be able to accept the limits on its voting power that would stem from embracing a more democratic governing principle for global institutions?

Ultimately, trying to sustain unsustainable agricultural or high social security subsidies and to limit international mergers and acquisitions (M&A), or even freedom of speech[1] will not only cause potential conflicts with some key European values, but, fail to protect Europe from the risks facing it.

Protectionist tendencies – economic or cultural - are likely to delay, and therefore raise the costs, of subsequent structural reform. Enlargement fatigue will surely cause Europe to lose momentum as a model for global governance.

Europe should adopt an offensive, not defensive, approach: continuing enlargement to export its values and systems and at the same time clearly demonstrating its commitment to these values by its actions, avoiding double standards for short-term interests.

The EU has the potential for global leadership, not by virtue of size or strength, but by being an example. However, the EU must orient itself towards improving the world in line with its own values, instead of its current self-centered, protectionist approach. Only in such a way can Europe deal with the risks it faces itself – let alone help the process of mitigating global risks.

Taking Opportunity

There is an **opportunity** for the EU for global leadership. Since 9/11 the world has been subjected to unilateralist policies; global sentiment has moved against the accumulation of power in a single country.

There is a growing wish for an alternative approach to global leadership; one not based on power, but on values.

Building Power

In order for the EU to exercise leadership, it also has to have sufficient power, defined in five dimensions: political, economic, sociological, technological, and military. As a **political** project, the EU is an innovation where countries, without recourse to force, agree to share sovereignty. However, it has become clear that both the efficiency and legitimacy of EU decision-making needs to be improved. Both administrative systems and individual perspectives need a more global dimension to deal with future global and European risks. The EU can be a global model, but only if the efficiency of decision-making takes precedence over protection of existing power equilibrium.

The EU is the premier global **economic** bloc, but competitiveness must be enhanced. Can the EU's present welfare mentality be maintained? From the point of economic development, the Lisbon goals carry a lot of weight. Failing to reach them will pose a major threat to aspirations of global leadership.

Sociologically, much store is set in Europe by "unity in diversity." Tolerance and understanding is too often only for current citizens; nationalism and rejection of "the other" are growing trends, as witnessed by immigration policies and attitudes to enlargement. Recent initiatives against the Roma people in France indicate that this "other" concept is taking root even within the EU. Another indication is the increasing xenophobia in Germany

Technologically, there are a number of constraints. The EU has collectively made some significant advances – adopting the Global System for Mobile Communications (GSM) standard or implementing common projects in the Seventh Framework Program. However, financing for innovation and the spirit of entrepreneurialism, remains weak. Also, due to an ageing and declining population the overcapacity in Europe's education systems is increasing, thereby reducing the motivation to upgrade them. Increasing foreign student registrations to European educational institutions will not only increase the competitive tension within these schools for better performance of existing students, but also allow further investments and potential to attract young people who develop with European values for the future.

Militarily, Europe lags well behind. Even in an era when world leadership depends less on military prowess, it is vital to share more significant military responsibility in conflict regions of the world. The EU itself is a successful peace project and should focus on exporting this idea.

Creating Vision

In addition to **opportunity** and **power**, leadership demands **vision**. One very important message should be conveyed to Europe's people: Europe should not be about protecting interests, but creating a structure by which European values become a global norm. This requires consistency between words and deeds in all EU actions. "European" values as democracy, human rights, rule of law, multiculturalism, protection of minorities, and laicism have to be applied consistently to gain the trust of global citizens. Defense of self-interest, alienation of "the other," fears over migration, worries over innovations such as genetically modified foods, and protection of shorter working hours will not allow the EU to maintain its existing prosperity, let alone attain global leadership to deal with global risks.

A True Test of Values: Approach to Membership of Turkiye

To the surprise of many, after forty years of courting, Turkiye successfully completed many reforms and secured negotiations for accession to the European Union. However, the recent developments in the negotiations is failing to create an impression of mutually trusting future partners, but one of European reluctance to accept Turkiye as an equal partner. Unless this changes significantly, it will be difficult to proceed on a win-win basis. This process will turn into one side establishing ever changing goal-posts and the other feeling alienated.

Yet Europe and Turkiye have a historical opportunity to throw out the prejudices of ages, discredit the "clash of civilizations," and establish a stronger EU. Turkish membership presents the potential to mitigate some of the key risks for Europe, *and* help the EU to be a role model for global governance.

Overcoming regional political risks can only be achieved if economic development spreads. Throughout the region, Turkiye is likely to be an engine of growth. As one observer put it, "Turkiye will be the 'Viagra' for Europe" by becoming the key agent to help improve European and regional competitiveness.

A win-win approach on Turkiye will be the key to addressing European risks, and making the EU a values-based global leader. Managing Turkiye's relationship with Europe relies on navigating the (sometimes false) dilemma.

Good governance requires wisdom. Sufist philosophy, which has an important place in Anatolian tradition, gives important advice. This philosophy, based on "tolerance" and "harmony," defines good governance as self-management. Good governance is to free ourselves from our fears, opening our eyes and hearts to new perspectives, to "regard others, as we regard ourselves." Individuals, civil society, political statesmen, businessmen, and managers of international organizations have critical roles in accomplishing that goal.

GLOBAL US: STRENGTH ERODES WITH UNILATERALISM

Since 9/11, the US unilateralism has been widely interpreted as a projection of hard power to enhance its own interests, rather than defending and disseminating values such as human rights, democracy, secularism, freedom of trade, and liberal economy. This had the result of diminishing goodwill of the global citizens.

No one can dispute the US's role as the only superpower of the world. In addition, the gap between the might of the US and those of her followers is so significant that the US may maintain such a position of power during our lifetime. However, erosion of goodwill in winning the hearts and minds of world citizens is very costly, even for the only superpower. For example, polls taken after Iraqi operations clearly indicated that the US brands were under the threat of rising anti-Americanism throughout the world. Perhaps more important is the spread of terrorism that is becoming more difficult to contain without winning the hearts and minds of people from different civilizations.

Turkiye, a long standing friend and ally of the US, sincerely shares common values such as human rights, democracy, secularism, free trade, and a liberal economic system with the US. Furthermore, her tradition of managing different civilizations under the Ottoman Empire presents an opportunity for a serious partnership to demonstrate that civilizations can and do share common values. Anatolia has been a melting pot of cultures, for a much longer period than the US.

During the twenty-first century, organized crime networks gained global dimensions in traffic of drugs, arms, humans, and organs. Mankind is under threat from chemical, biological, and nuclear weapons of mass destruction. In the future, we may have to protect ourselves from Spatial threats. Understandably, the superpower of the world, the US, is taking actions to preempt such threats. However, those actions will be more effective if taken jointly with other nations sharing similar values and if they are targeted not only to the threats themselves, but also to their root causes. Turkiye's position as the only secularly and democratically governed Muslim-populated country, its experience in fighting terror, as a reliable ally, her military prowess, and deep experience in managing diverse and wide areas puts her in a special position to enhance the strategic vision of promoting democracy, freedom, and liberal economy.

To deal with global threats, we need legitimate, global cooperation based on globally consistent principles. To be globally consistent will mean that we should start implementing common values in all aspects of life. This is not as easy as it sounds. Yet, this is exactly what the single superpower of the world has to do. Preaching free trade, but protecting uncompetitive local industries; promoting human rights, but dismissing Ebu Garib and Guantanamo Bay; exporting global rules and regulations, but taking exceptions from Kyoto Agreements and jurisdiction of International Criminal Court does not help the credibility of promoting common values throughout the world.

In short, US unilateralism does not fit well with the US' values. Ignoring respect for people and freedoms even when they are not US citizens, or even the existence of such a perception begins to erode the moral superiority of the US. The most powerful nation in the world has to understand that sound governance is serving all humans, not merely the strong.

For sustainable development and peace on earth, the US has to comprehend how her decisions impact on others and understand that good governance is, in fact, self-governance. To ensure sustainability of peace and stability, the US has to guard the values that made the US a superpower and apply them consistently not only within her own borders, but also globally. In an increasingly transparent world, inconsistencies cannot be sustained, at least morally. Hence, the US has to demonstrate a level of wisdom and "regard others, as she regards her own citizens and her own interests."

GLOBAL NATO: GLOBAL SECURITY INFRASTRUCTURE NEEDS GLOBAL GOVERNANCE

The most important role of government is to provide security and maintain stability. Significant changes occurred in the perception of global threat especially after September 11. People no longer need a government to declare war. Communities with indefinite identities, borders, and power (namely terrorists) start a war against a nation who has the most powerful military force.

Organized crime networks gain global dimensions in the traffic of drugs, arms, humans, and organs. Mankind is under threat from chemical, biological, and nuclear weapons of mass destruction. Mankind may also have to protect itself against threats from Space.

Globalization of threats has common root causes:

1. Ease of attaining technology. Big governments started to lose their monopoly in many areas as a result of technological developments (like biological weapons), and they are trying to preserve their superiority in other areas through international agreements.
2. Imbalances on earth. About one-fifth of people living on earth are trying to survive with US$1 a day income, whereas nearly half of them manage with US$2 a day. Developed countries spend $600 billion on military; provide agricultural subsidies of around US$300 billion, while their foreign aid budgets total less than US$60 billion. Furthermore the proportion of humans living in developed countries is decreasing every year.
3. Another imbalance example arises on use of water, which forms the basis of life. An average person needs 5 liters of water daily in order to survive, and needs 50 liters of water when other vital activities such as cooking and washing are taken into consideration. However, while an American citizen consumes 250–300 liters of water daily, one in five people around the world (20%) do not have access to clean safe water. Each year more than 5 million people die as a result of diseases caused by lack of access to water (ten times the number of people lost in wars.) A similar situation is relevant on world energy utilization. The refusal of the highest per capita user of energy to participate in the Kyoto Protocol causes reactions. The US is seen as the biggest contributor to global warming and is one of the countries with the cheapest energy utilization.
4. Developments in communication technology. Developments in technology are bringing the dictum of "God sees everything" into reality by enabling "The global society to see everything." Information not given through CNN reaches people through Al Jazeera; information not provided there reaches wide communities through the Internet (where available). Consequently, all personal, corporate, and social secrets disappear, an example being the Wikileaks incident. The period of superiority gained by those with information shortens. Whether we like it or not, technological developments and a democratic way of life increase transparency in all aspects of life. Increased transparency forces communities to be consistent in both internal and external principles.

In summary, governments, no matter how much power they have, will not be able to deal with globalized threats on their own.

Consequently, it is essential to organize on a global scale to deal with global threats.

Can NATO, organized during the Cold War, renew itself in this environment and transform itself into a global security system? For this, important changes are needed, especially in minds and social processes:

1. Security is no longer a service that can only be provided by defense forces. In an environment where interdependencies of people increase, the security of networks is a responsibility of all members of these networks. Therefore, threat consciousness and defense responsibility of each member of the society should be increased rather than keeping threat and defense strategies confidential and in the realm of the few who are assigned to protect us.
2. Different governmental units should share the security responsibility. For example, the ministry of health, municipality service providers, and regulatory agencies in critical areas such as telecommunication services should work cooperatively to provide security.
3. A healthy security system needs support from the business world and civil society organizations. For this reason, we have to restructure our processes to increase the understanding of security issues by unconventional parties, from the strategy development stages to the implementation stages.
4. To deal with global threats, we need legitimate, global institutions that work with globally consistent principles.

To be globally consistent will mean that mankind should start implementing common values in all aspects of life. This is not as easy as it sounds. For example, can the world accept a "one man – one vote" principle that is the practice within national boundaries to be applied in global affairs? Would this bring global legitimacy? Or, should each country's vote be equal on global system regardless of its size? Or, should countries be able to vote according to their military power? Or should governments and/or companies and/or people be given voting rights according to their economic strength? In that case, how should changes in these strengths over time be managed in order to secure the legitimacy of a global system? Can another approach be to accept the US, which has established a clear superiority in military capabilities, to decide and implement global issues on its own? If so, to gain global legitimacy, should a portion of the votes, say 20%, for US Presidency be given by citizens of other countries?

If the international organizations formed after World War II – United Nations, World Bank, IMF, World Trade Organization, and NATO – were able to restructure themselves around the world's new needs, without losing their decision making, implementation skills and legitimacy, these issues could be solved in a transparent process. Similarly if the EU is to be a sustainable global example, its new constitution should be established through an open and transparent process based on universal principles, not with a view to protecting current political balances.

NATO, with its past experiences, decision making infrastructure, common language tradition, powerful investments, and its experience in providing peace and stability, is a candidate for constituting a legitimate base for global security. Meanwhile, for NATO's mission to gain a global dimension, its decision mechanisms should also gain a global dimension. For example, an institution, where India and China are not involved in decision making mechanisms, will have significant difficulties in achieving global legitimacy.

In summary, as topics about our daily life gain global characteristics, our vision, organizations, and management systems should also gain a global perspective. As the world becomes more interconnected, we have to understand that the problems of others are also our own. Therefore, we have to make sure that good governance principles are applied throughout our management structures and systems.

Good management is building mutual trust with consistent behavior. Good management requires a wisdom that reflects real justice. "Sufism" philosophy, which has an important place in Anatolian tradition, gives us important clues on this issue. This philosophy based on "tolerance" and "harmony" defines good management as managing ourselves. Good management is to free ourselves from our fears, opening our eyes and hearts to new perspectives.

The real legitimacy will be gained only if people have a say about shaping their own future – to contribute in the global decision making process. This transformation is also in the basis of change from "management concept" to "governance concept," which means involvement and mutuality. For sustainable development and world peace, we should understand how our decisions affect others and reach an enhanced level of wisdom that will reduce our selfishness. Individuals, civil society organizations, statesmen, and managers of international organizations will have critical roles in accomplishing a sustainable world order that is just and based on the universal principle of regarding others, as we regard ourselves. If we are successful in bringing democratic principles to the solution of global issues, with the inclusion of all interested parties in global decision making, we will help achieve a secure world.

A GLOBAL ISSUE: WATER IS IN NEED OF GOVERNANCE

Water is life. Everywhere and every day we need it. Water has the power to move millions of people. People move when there is too little of it and they move when there is too much of it. People love water, they sing, dance, and pray for water. They even pay to look at it, as evidenced by the values of water front properties.

The shortages and contamination of fresh water, the basis for all forms of life, are among the world's most important problems. Solutions to the problems of over-exploitation and pollution of water require a consensus regarding the governance of 300 water basins that are shared by two or more nations, covering 50% of the land surface of the globe where more than 40% of the people live.

Water use has grown exponentially in modern times. In the first 80 years of the twentieth century the world's average per capita water use increased by 200%. This accounted to a 566% increase in withdrawals from freshwater sources. A significant portion of these resources are now unusable due to industrial and agricultural pollution. Since all life depends on water, present trends of water waste and pollution threaten the world's basic life support systems.

History provides ample evidence of ancient cities, such as Babylon, Persepolis, and Fatehpur Sikri that used up their available water and perished. Overused aquifers cause a loss of biodiversity. China's famous Yellow River failed to reach the sea for more than 220 days in 1997. In China at least 50 cities face acute shortages as the water table drops by 1 to 2 meters a year. In Jakarta and Bangkok, excessive pumping of groundwater has led to intrusion of seawater into the aquifers.

The average person needs five liters of water to survive. The minimum amount of water needed for drinking, cooking, bathing, and sanitation is 50 liters per day. An average person in the US uses 250 to 300 liters per day for the same tasks. One in five people living today (1.2 billion) does not have access to safe drinking water, and half the world's population does not have adequate sanitation. More than five million people die each year from water related diseases, 10 times the number killed in wars. By 2025, two thirds of world's people will live in countries with water shortages.

If we believe in human rights, we should also accept the principle that every human has the right to an essential minimum amount of water to sustain life and meet basic sanitation needs. At the Rio Earth Summit the rights of all human beings to their basic daily water requirements were expanded to include measures needed to preserve ecosystems.

The Fifth World Water Forum, held in Istanbul, focused on how to manage water resources – a very difficult question. In most societies water is not a part of the market mechanisms that ensure efficient exploitation and utilization of resources. Sharing of water was one of the first elements in the progress towards communal living. It also has cultural and spiritual significance that requires special care in its governance.

Issues regarding basic human needs, resource sustainability, and natural habitat conservation provide a case for government intervention for establishing the policy and legislative and regulatory frameworks for managing water supply and demand. However, we should also recognize that markets provide the best mechanism to promote efficiency and when deregulation and innovation come together, the results can be startling, as evidenced by the electricity and telecommunications industries.

Water is such a basic need that many think that water is nature's gift and should be free. However, that very same nature left it to someone else to drive the well, dam the river, lay the pipes, power the pumps, and add the chemicals to bring clean water to where we live. Water is indeed a human right, but it is a great mistake to equate such a right to be without costs. **Every right has a corresponding obligation**, responsibility, and cost. Artificially low water prices are self defeating, resulting in deteriorating infrastructure and an inefficient service.

Inefficient use of water is often initiated and reinforced by government subsidies. Attendant water rights, whether formal or informal are jealously defended by privileged users. Water allocations often become locked into clearly low return uses (such as irrigation), which in turn results in high economic costs for high-return needs (such as urban utilization). Such inefficient allocations often result in non-transparent subsidies of significant magnitudes.

For example, 70% of water withdrawals are for irrigation and are often heavily subsidized. As much as 60% of the water allocated for irrigation is lost through leakage and evaporation before it even reaches the crop, and an additional 20% may be lost at the field. There are very few incentives to improve the efficiency of water delivery when water is free or very under-priced.

However, people are recognizing that water has a real market value. Conservationists rightly believe that too often the value of a natural resource is under-represented. This has led to significant inefficiencies in water use and production, and reduces environmental sustainability.

Users and polluters of water should pay: to ensure environmental sustainability; for the mobilization of necessary capital for water infrastructure (estimated need is between US\$70–180 billion annually); to promote efficiency improving innovations; and to empower communities (with direct subsidies whenever necessary) to promote participatory democracy.

Beyond the basic needs for human wellbeing and environmental renewal, scarcity of water is largely an economic issue. **The idea that water has an economic value** in all its competing uses **should underlie all efforts in rational water resource management**. Treating water as a tradable commodity should bring greater efficiency and productivity in its use.

The mobility of water through the hydrological cycle has made it difficult to establish ownership and control rights. However, one of the first elements of establishing market mechanisms is through establishing property rights. Conditions for trading water require a clear definition of water rights that does not, currently, exist in most countries.

Institutional arrangements should be put in place to allow the emergence of international water markets. Economic interdependence based on water trade will help avoid conflict. Innovation prompted by market forces can contribute to improving the quantity and quality of water. Technologies are available that could cut water demand by 40 to 90% in industry, 30% in cities and 10 to 50% in agriculture without reducing economic output or the quality of life.

Governments have dominated water policy making. Recently however, NGOs have taken an active role in advocacy, fieldwork, capacity building, and research. NGOs help bring legitimacy through society's involvement; they bring innovation, monitoring (as in the case of human rights), and through research, free availability of information. Civil society is taking an ever increasing role in poverty alleviation and improving the quality of life by helping people secure access to safe and affordable water and sanitation.

Success in public policy making would be increasingly difficult, if one misses the significance of this transformation. This is so because the international community and NGOs are instrumental in shaping global standards, gathering and disseminating information that feeds decision making, and in problem solving. Most importantly they bring participatory democracy to life. They also help establish new markets and innovative implementation mechanisms. The task of the international community and NGOs is not to replace elected representatives or governmental organizations, but to support and improve their performance through a participatory approach.

Surmounting the issues related to this vital element, water, requires a common understanding and joint decision making at the international, regional, sectorial, and stakeholder levels. For such a participatory decision making all stakeholders, including women and minorities, must have a voice.

The gender division of labor in many societies allocates to women the responsibility for collecting and storing water, and maintaining sanitation. Providing clean and dependable water close to home can substantially reduce women's home workloads and enable them to participate more meaningfully in economic activities. Recently women in a Turkish village made a collective protest to abstain from sex until their husbands ensured that sufficient investment was found to bring water to the village. And it worked!!

Concepts like **a global water tax** on each person who uses more than 50 liters per day should be introduced to pay for providing water to those that do not have access to clean water at a rate of their overuse. This would mean that an average world citizen, who uses five times as much as the minimum daily requirement, would pay for four deprived individual's access to clean water, until each human being gains access to a minimum of 50 liters per day.

Human beings' mutual interdependence is ever increasing as we all share the fate of this common earth. We should all recognize that the exploitation of a global resource, such as water, requires global decision making and caring for others. We should also recognize that technological developments will continually force us to behave in a more responsible way. For example, advances in communication technologies imply that inconsistencies, whether personal, corporate, or social, are no longer sustainable. Technological developments and freedom of thought accompanying democratic governments lead to transparency in management. **Increasing transparency** in turn **forces societies to be consistent** in both internal and external policies.

Higher transparency also leads people and institutions to be consistent in their behavior. Sound management is built on the nurturing of mutual trust by consistent behavior. It requires a certain wisdom reflecting true justice. This philosophy is best summarized by Yunus Emre, the great poet and thinker of the thirteenth century, who advised "Regard the other, as you regard yourself, this is the meaning of four holy books, if there is any."

What matters is the **participation of people in the global decision making processes shaping their own future**. This transformation lies at the heart of the change of focus from management to governance, emphasizing participation and mutuality. A major prerequisite to such a participative management approach is that large masses be interested in the incidents affecting their lives, have the necessary information, and possess the tools to participate in decision making. To this end, they must belong to the information age and access information technologies. It is a global responsibility to make the necessary steps to satisfy these needs. It is an overarching responsibility that crosses national boundaries, one to be assumed by the international community as a whole.

If we are to solve the global water issue or other issues relevant to the future of human kind, and if we really believe in human rights and democracy, we should strive for the education of all the people of this planet and to instill the "world citizen" notion, and ensure their participation in decision making processes. We have to understand that **sound governance is serving all humans, not merely the strong**.

For **sustainable development and peace on earth**, we must recognize how our decisions impact on others. We must understand that good governance is, in fact, self-governance. To ensure sustainability of water and life on earth we should reach a level of wisdom where we open our eyes and hearts to new perspectives, and "regard others, as we regard ourselves."

In short, whichever perspective we may take, whether the perspective of leading global players such as the EU and the US; or the perspective of a global institution such as NATO, or the perspective of a global issue such as effective utilization of water, the key element to reaching a sustainable global governance requires a shift in attitudes of both the leaders as well as the citizens of our globe.

NOTE

1 Such as the French Parliament initiative that conflicts with freedom of thought and speech regarding prohibition of denying the Armenian claim of identifying the events of 1914–1916 as "genocide," which Turkiye and Turkish people vehemently oppose or a similar approach that was enacted in Switzerland. As this book was going to publication the French Parliament has finally defeated this initiative after keeping it on its agenda for four years.

CHAPTER 4

Effective Public Policy Making and Administration

Trust is the foundation of development.

'No legacy is so rich as honesty.' (William Shakespeare)

Today, individuals' urge to shape their future collectively is greater than ever. Their quest for new ways of governance is leading to fundamental changes whereby individuals, private and public institutions try to harmonize their diverse interests through complicated interactive decision making processes. While the relationship between citizens and public administration is being restructured in today's world, the concept of "governance" is also going through a transformation. The new "governance" concept entails a mutual interaction between the government and the citizens.

"Governance" signifies a transformation from a type of relationship where one side governs the other to a set of relationships where mutual interaction takes place in order to find the most desirable choices for the citizens. Thus, governance forms the political, economic, and administrative power that societies use to administer their activities. It involves the mechanisms, processes, and institutions that citizens, groups, and societies utilize in joint decision-making and implementation, in expressing their interest and in fulfilling their obligations as well as solving conflicts. In this context, governance points to the nature of mutual interaction among social actors as well as between social actors and public administration, and it encapsulates the meaning of "participative decision making."

In the past, the issues affecting public life used to be decided jointly by those with a right to vote. **Democracy**, which could be considered as **"participatory"** in this understanding, eventually turned into **"representative"** democracy; because both the number of participants, and the complexity and diversity of the decisions have increased. However, as from time to time representatives' interests did not overlap with societal interests (the "agency problem") and citizens' willingness to participate in the decisions that influenced their lives has, as a result of technological developments in the field of education and communication increased. This trend has been reversed in the twenty-first century and a new form of participatory democracy has started to gain importance. Hence, **civil society organizations have begun to play a role in taking societal decisions together with the elected.**

The role of the state is under constant debate with changing global economic, social, and political conditions. Widespread adoption of democracy as the preferred form of government, and of the market economy as the preferred economic system points to a need for clear definitions of control and responsibility in the provision of public services. The terms and efficiency of state involvement have a direct bearing on the institution of a competitive environment, and on equitable welfare and income distribution. Therefore citizens also expect the state to make the most efficient use of its resources to their benefit.

The quality of public administration determines the environment within which the individual, companies, and NGOs function. Therefore the effectiveness of state authority is essential when increasing the welfare of society at large in a balanced manner. **Good governance is the main methodology to improve the quality of decisions taken and therefore to improve the quality of life through more effective use of public resources.**

BASIC FUNCTIONS OF THE STATE

It is widely recognized that state authority is necessary in the following seven categories:

1. to ensure proper functioning of the rule of law;
2. to establish the necessary framework for macroeconomic stability and a fair competitive environment;
3. to ensure adequate investment into fundamental infrastructure, education, health, and social security programs;
4. to secure the rights of the certain weaker segments of society that need protection, such as children, the disabled, or the elderly;
5. to protect the rights of future generations in matters such as the environment and cultural heritage;
6. to maintain domestic security;
7. to defend the country against external threats.

In addition to these recognized categories where state authority is deemed necessary, the emerging preferred role for the state is to be limited to that of regulation and supervision. The key goal of the state is to establish a fair playground to motivate individuals and companies to innovate and improve the quality of life. Direct intervention is acceptable only in cases where markets cannot efficiently function. In cases where the state is both a player and the referee, it becomes difficult to establish conditions conducive to increasing overall welfare, productivity goes down, and there is room for populism motivated deterioration. Therefore, the accepted norm is becoming for the state to be referee only.

As the function of the modern state comes to be confined to the above categories, the beneficiary of its services is also fundamentally redefined. The state is expected to regard its citizens not as "subjects" but as "clients."

In this process, a new understanding that accepts the individual as a partner of the public administration is gradually emerging. This new status of the individual is referred to as "stakeholder." Consequently, the status of the individual in government (laid out as "partner" in the 1992 Rio Summit) has turned into "stakeholder" in the Habitat II Conference convened in Istanbul in 1996. As a result of these developments, instead of a type of public administration that perceives the relationship between the state and the citizen mostly as hierarchical, the concept of "governance" has emerged that denotes joint decision-making by the public administration and the stakeholders, and where the public administration is accountable to the individual alongside the state.

GOVERNANCE IN THE PUBLIC SECTOR

Public administration within the concept of governance entails a cheaper, high quality and effective service provision as well as a participatory, accountable, and transparent government. In the new millennium, societies are attempting creative and productive forms of governance, and learning from their experiences. A new form of citizenship awareness is in the making. This new identity demands higher standards, yet shows ownership of its problems and partakes in the creation of these higher standards, introducing the solutions and setting up the structures.

Good governance at the public level depends on the ability of state organs and public service organizations to encourage participation. It also depends on a consistent, transparent, and accountable public administration that ensures the fairness and effectiveness of decisions and their implementation.

Taking participation, predictability, and transparency into account in the formulation of public policies ensures their legitimacy. Only in this manner will public policies turn out to be citizen-oriented and effective.

WHAT DOES GOOD GOVERNANCE DO?

Good governance should:

1. bring public administration closer to the citizen;
2. make public administration more effective by continuously improving the quality of public service;
3. ensure corruption is combated;
4. ensure the participation of different stakeholders in government by voicing their opinion, which enriches the content of the decisions and improves the effectiveness of their implementation;
5. strengthen democracy;
6. improve the legitimacy of institutions;
7. ensure that decisions and processes are open and understandable.

PRINCIPLES OF GOVERNANCE

The basic principles of governance are: Consistency (predictability and adherence to law), Responsibility, Accountability, Fairness, Transparency, Effectiveness and proportionality, and Deployment (participation and subsidiarity). The **CRAFTED** principles of governance.

Consistency refers to consistency of decisions both in reference to one another and also over time. The government takes decisions based on objective information, that these decisions are within the rule of law, and that these are supervised through legal channels. Consistency makes for a predictable regulatory environment in which citizens can make long-term development and investment decisions.

Responsibility refers to the ability of the state authority to have the capacity and flexibility to respond rapidly to social changes.

Accountability refers to the necessity for public officials to use public resources responsibly, to account for how these resources are budgeted and utilized, and to report on the process.

Fairness ensures that decisions of the public sector do not result in unbalanced benefits to any segment of the society, that the rules all citizens are subject to are openly and clearly laid out, and that they are applied uniformly to everyone. Fairness reinforces the confidence of citizens in the state.

Transparency indicates that public officials carry out decision-making processes and their implementation in an open manner and share them with other stakeholders.

Effectiveness and proportionality indicates that the implementation of decisions taken by the government applies equally to everyone simultaneously and that there is a reasonable correlation among the results to be achieved, the resources to be used, and their negative impact on certain groups.

Deployment indicates that the preparation, implementation, and monitoring stages of the decision-making process involve effective participation of civil society organizations and the public at large, starting with the individual. Taking public decisions in a participatory manner by involving all stakeholders to be affected by that particular decision facilitates its implementation.

Governance in public administration indicates that the decision-making process is carried out in cooperation with the participation of all stakeholders and that administrator's act in a conciliatory, transparent, accountable, effective, and responsible manner. In other words, government is run not only by a group of elected officials but also with the involvement of other types of groups such as civil society organizations, professional chambers, private sector organizations, universities, and so forth. Within the concept of governance, it is expected that decisions are taken in a manner open to the public and that all stakeholders are involved in the process, demonstrating a government model based on information and consensus.

FROM REPRESENTATIVE DEMOCRACY TO PARTICIPATIVE DEMOCRACY

In a world where global citizenship is becoming prominent, neither human rights nor democracy is perceived limited to their traditional meanings. Traditional human rights rise on the main principle that no person should be discriminated against their gender, color, race, language, religion, social class or political views. Similarly, democracy is generally defined as right to vote, freedom of expression and related rights.

However, nowadays both human rights and democracy are outgrowing these concepts. Now what matters is the participation of people in the global decision making processes shaping their own future. This transformation lies at the heart of the change of focus from management to governance, emphasizing participation and mutuality.

It is becoming more and more important for governments to perceive this transformation. International community and civil society organizations take on more of a role in shaping the standards, gathering and dissemination of the information that feeds decision making and problem solving, and therefore advancing and compelling participatory democracy. It must also be remembered that the role of civil society organizations is not to replace the elected officials or public organizations, but to challenge them with a participatory approach in order to support and improve their functioning.

INCREASING EFFECTIVENESS REQUIRES A PARTICIPATIVE APPROACH

While a reduced role of the state is becoming the norm globally, even in developed countries, the public sector accounts for a minimum of 30% of their economies. Considering also the impact on the remaining 70% in terms of regulation, public administration has a determining role in the lives of its citizens, and its efficient functioning is critical. The fundamental issue is not seeking a "minimal" state, but rather for a "lean" and "effective" state. To achieve effectiveness, policy makers have to adopt a participative approach to determining their regulatory and supervisory methods, take advantage of competitive market mechanisms, and develop the mechanisms to solicit feedback from the stakeholders in determining priorities. Participative democracy is the key to effectiveness.

To increase the level of welfare in society, the concepts of thrift, productivity, and effectiveness should extend to all aspects of social life, and in utilization of public resources in particular. Since it is not possible to improve performance if it is not measured, it is also important to carry out periodical impact analyses of the adopted policies and to share the results with the public. The quality of participatory democracy is increased with the quality of the feedback provided to the policy formulation process and with the prevalence of participation.

REGULATORY IMPACT ANALYSIS IS THE KEY TO LEARNING AND IMPROVING

Effective and productive use of public resources is a priority issue for development of any country. Politics is based on the bid to take on the right and responsibility of decision making on utilization of public resources. Even though there will be different priorities between various segments of society as to the "correct" allocation of these resources, the major impediment to the correct allocation stems not from these differences but from inadequate employment of management science in public administration. Therefore, it is critical for politicians to be inclined to focus not only on priorities but also on governance issues that incorporate attendant processes.

The basic expectation of people, from their government systems, is an improvement in their quality of life. One of the pitfalls of representative democracy is the potential for the interests of the representatives of the voters and that of the voters themselves not always being aligned. Therefore the appeal of participatory democracy is increasing, bringing with it increasing management quality.

One of the best ways of evaluating the impacts of public administration decisions is regulatory impact analysis. Performance that cannot be measured cannot be improved. Therefore, carrying out periodical impact analysis of implemented policies and sharing the results with the public is gaining importance.

Regulatory impact analysis is a methodological assessment of impact of current or draft regulation. The market consequences of decisions taken within the regulatory and supervisory powers of the state are very important. Universal applications show that there are different scales of regulatory impact analysis. Some countries have institutions that oversee the quality of regulatory impact analysis, and more importantly, that provide the principle guidelines for regulatory impact analysis. These institutions also provide consulting and technical support, oversee the quality of the analysis, and report on how closely the guidelines are followed.

A fundamental means of increasing the quality of public sector decisions is to steer the decision makers toward scientific methods. Therefore, developing a culture of impartial and fair evaluation of the impact of decisions both prior to and post decision-taking will result in an improvement of the quality of life of citizens. This is why it is important to measure the present or potential impact of public policy decisions, learn from them, and incorporate a culture of learning to public administration.

Using regulatory impact analysis to measure the results of public policy was enacted into law in the US in 1975, in the EU in 1995, and in Turkiye in 2007. However, such analyses are yet to be used widely. Leading NGOs are lagging behind in conducting regulatory impact analysis and in the sharing of the results with decision makers and public.

Different methods are employed in public decision making. Decisions are made:

- by experts on particular subjects;
- by consensus among related parties;
- by politicians;
- by taking best practices examples from other countries;
- by benefiting from prior applications.

As public policy decisions are multidimensional, and impact different segments differently, regulatory impact analysis is important but complicated. However, regulatory impact analyses are very beneficial in:

- understanding the costs and benefits of public decisions;
- interaction and coordination with various other decisions;
- the participation of the public or well informed NGOs in the process;
- the development of accountability.

Carrying out the following stages in public decision making proves advantageous:

1. defining the issue under consideration and sharing it with the stakeholders;
2. determining the policy targets;
3. determining the segments that will be impacted by the policy;
4. identifying alternative policies;
5. conducting regulatory impact analysis for the alternative policies;
6. sharing the results of regulatory impact analysis with related segments and soliciting feedback;
7. selecting the policy alternative and determining punitive sanctions;
8. determining the parameters for impact analysis once the policy is in practice and measuring them;
9. assessing the measured results and making the necessary policy changes if necessary.

Parties involved in the public decision making take into account the following considerations:

- has the issue been defined accurately?
- is state involvement necessary for addressing the issue?
- is the best option for intervention a new rule or regulation?
- does the decision making body have legal authority?
- is the cost-benefit of the regulation and its follow up reasonable?
- is the impact of the regulation sufficiently grasped by the related segments?
- have the inputs by the related segments been taken into account?
- how will compliance of related segments be fairly achieved?

In summary, the principle "performance that cannot be measured cannot be improved" is valid for public policy as well. Therefore regulatory impact analysis is an important management tool for the improvement of the quality of decision making, in enabling participative democracy, and in ensuring ongoing development and learning.

ETHICAL VALUES ARE KEY TO GOOD GOVERNANCE

Creating added value, increasing welfare, and improving quality of life necessitates improved management quality. The basic principle of such improvement is managing by values. For good public administration, the principle involves taking economically rational, productive, efficient, and ethical decisions, and actively implementing them.

Ethical values refer to behavior in line with societal norms and expectations beyond those dictated by law. The experiences of countries identify the following conditions necessary to set up a sound "ethical infrastructure":

1. political decisiveness and exemplary behavior by the elected;
2. an influential and well-organized civil society;
3. instituting effective processes for accountability;
4. establishing business ethics guidelines that are not restrictive and communicating these;
5. establishing effective training for civil servants and setting up processes for best practices comparisons;
6. provision of a suitable working environment;
7. a sound legal infrastructure.

EARNING PUBLIC TRUST

Genuine adherence to ethical values can serve as the vehicle to overcome mistrust people have in public administration. Accountability is necessary to earn public trust. Some recommendations to actively promote accountability can be listed as follows:

- keeping written records;
- establishing result and purpose oriented control mechanisms;
- establishing support mechanisms with NGOs;
- instituting processes that encourage whistle blowing on unethical behavior with appropriate protection for the informants;
- mandatory disclosure of personal assets and relationships for civil servants.

While effective control mechanisms for adhering to ethical values is important, it is also widely recognized that punitive measures without proper evaluation make for public sector managers that are frozen into inaction and unable to take the necessary measures for the efficient use of public resources. Adherence to ethical behavior cannot only be achieved by control mechanisms, but also by appropriate incentive mechanisms. Employing control mechanisms with a view to improving the processes, encouraging ethical behavior, and targeting improved performance are important in sustaining the new public sector management approach. Ethical values are the most important tool for politicians and civil servants in order to maintain their integrity.

Everyone that has access to and say over others' resources has to gain their trust. To gain trust, there are seven principles that not only private sector or NGO managers but also elected officials and public servants have to observe:

1. they should hold the public interest above their own;
2. they should maintain financial independence;
3. they should maintain impartiality;
4. they should maintain accountability;
5. they should maintain transparency;
6. they should maintain honesty and openness;
7. they should support the above principles by living by them.

To hold the public interest above their own means not obtaining financial benefits above and beyond what is assigned to the particular position. This extends to the manager not providing any special benefits to anyone in his immediate circle or even to those who bring him to his particular position.

To maintain financial independence means that people who put themselves in the position of depending on others financially also make themselves open to manipulation that is in conflict with public interest. Regardless of their intentions, it is important for people not to be put in such a situation. In 1993 Pierre Beregovoy, the French Prime Minister known for his integrity, was drawn to suicide because he had borrowed money from a friend who could derive benefits from his policies. Providing even limited financial means to public officials by those who are in a position to benefit from their decisions should be prohibited in order not to risk loss of trust in public administration.

To maintain impartiality identifies the responsibility, in matters pertaining to public interest, for assigning positions or awarding contracts to those that are best qualified for the job at hand. If such elections, assignments, or contract awards are carried out with a biased mentality, then it means the people in those the positions will put the interests of those that elect or assign him or their circles before those of the mission of the institution that they lead. This leads to institutional failure and public mistrust. In societies lacking transparency and trust, choosing "one of us" is the primary criterion, which in turn leads to the deterioration of both public trust and public sector performance.

To maintain accountability requires that people in public management positions hold themselves open to investigation in order to gain public trust.

To maintain transparency requires the ability to support the decisions made and a willingness to share the reasoning with the public.

To maintain honesty and openness means that if public officials find themselves in situations where there might be an apparent conflict of interest in the decisions they have to take because of involvement of their immediate circle, they should declare this openly and leave themselves out of the decision-making process for that particular case.

To support the above principles by living by them means that leaders who adhere to the above principles as a way of life gain public trust and are successful in fulfilling the mission of their institutions. These leaders also set up precedents for people who follow them in office.

IMPORTANCE OF MERITOCRACY

In countries where transparency and trust are not prevailing, the main criterion for election is choosing "one of ours." This is leads to a vicious circle where people seeking public office or position rely only on who they know, rather than on learning and developing relevant skills and knowledge. This presents an impediment to the advancement of society.

Failure to appoint public officials according to meritocracy not only results in less effective public service, but also leads to cronyism, lack of improvement in public management systems, even corruption, and most importantly sends out the wrong signals to the community as a whole with regards to individuals' who are focusing on improving their capabilities. It becomes a social "cancer."

Yet, preferring to choose "one of us" rather than the "best person to do the job" is not always due to lack of goodwill. In many cases it is due to lack of sufficient management knowledge or effort. If one does not have a thorough understanding on the job to be done, it would be difficult to define who "the best person to do the job" would be. A person may then choose loyalty as the key characteristic as it would be preferable to hire someone who would follow orders as they are defined, at times inconsistently, along the way.

Also, those who have the capability to define what needs to be done from the beginning may be unable to choose the "best person" due to lack of effort. That is because choosing the "best" requires a fair and broad search process that takes effort and time.

Nevertheless, failing to aim for the best and opting for the familiar is a common sin in public administration that needs to be corrected for good governance.

Adherence to ethical standards and living by the above principles enhances good governance in the public sector and improves the quality of lives of the stakeholders as a whole. Perhaps as important, the governing and steering ability of the democratic system improves.

Trust requires freedom at its core. Freedom brings creativity and fulfillment. This is why trust is fundamental to development.

TAX REGIME: SIMPLICITY AND FAIRNESS INCREASE ADHERENCE

One of the important elements of sovereignty is the right to impose taxes. States that do not use this right in a responsible, just, and effective manner cannot earn the trust of their citizens, gain respect in the international arena, or manage their economies effectively. Historically and today, one of the most important measures of the effectiveness of a state is to determine whether it has a responsible, just, and effective tax administration.

Taxes are important on both a micro and a macro scale because of their size in the economy. Composition of taxes should be aligned with economic and social policies, global taxation trends, and should not deter competitiveness. Taxes should be collected to serve the taxpayer, be put to public use effectively, and the taxpayer should be willing.

Tax evasion and inability on the part of the state to include all taxpayers in the tax base results in unjust taxation. Such injustice stands in the way of entrepreneurship, and prevents new investment and employment. Moreover, if the tax base is not wide enough, it is not possible to reduce tax rates or to provide incentives for new investment and development.

Formulating tax policy or tax reform should:

1. incorporate mechanisms to solicit taxpayer input;
2. evaluate tax impact with economic modeling;
3. involve a transparent, open, accountable legislative process.

Tax administration should serve the taxpayer, simplify operations as best possible, and aim at sector specialization, and develop a cooperative approach. In structuring tax administration care should be taken to instill a culture of performance, to ensure continuity, and to continually develop institutional capabilities.

This is possible by instituting a national data infrastructure. An important aspect of establishing an e-state is maintaining up-to-date data. Considering that every commercial entity interacts with the tax office a few times each month, the importance of a current database is evident.

REGULATORY AND SUPERVISORY BODIES: RULE MAKING IS AN INTERACTIVE ART

The modern day understanding of state intervention in the economy is acceptable only in cases where market mechanisms cannot work effectively. These instances can be:

1. positive economic exogenous cases preventing adequate investment for social optimization;

2. negative economic exogenous factors;
3. imbalance of information;
4. natural monopolies.

In particular, these bodies are necessary in order to eliminate the short-comings of the supervisory authority with horizons limited to electoral periods in sectors that require long-term investment. Sector specialized regulatory and supervisory authority that is independent from political administration can remain immune to frequent political interventions.

The main purpose of regulatory and supervisory boards is to set up the necessary regulatory framework that will allow adequate investment and maintain fair competition, and protect consumers from unfair practices by market players. To this end, regulatory boards establish the rules, oversee and supervise compliance with their rules, investigate where necessary, and educate the market players.

For regulatory boards to carry out these functions effectively requires them to be independent, transparent, accountable, knowledgeable, and reliable. However, these concepts need to be clearly defined. Being knowledgeable and independent does not mean these boards will not be accountable.

Therefore, while the state is structured along the lines of regulatory and supervisory boards, the process of selection and appointment of the chairmen, members, or experts to these boards, how the structure separates the functions of rule making, decision making, and administering, and the board's relationship with the political administration, the judiciary, and the sector players need to be established transparently.

In appointments, experience, skill, and reliability of the members rather than proximity to any political party should be the norm. If the candidates proposed by political parties go through a transparent inquiry process that involves civil society representatives, the trust element will be significantly enhanced.

The principle of soliciting participation should apply to the regulatory boards as well. Input from chambers of trade and industry, professional groups, private sector companies that will be affected by the regulation and local representatives where appropriate will bring many advantages. If such participation is solicited in a transparent process, it will facilitate adaptation of the regulation and compliance.

These boards should also have performance criteria. The guiding principle for these criteria should be the creation of an effective regulatory environment. As an example, an energy market regulatory board should have as its target the achievement of energy price levels that are compatible and competitive in relation to global levels, and to ensure energy availability where there is demand, at the most reasonable cost.

A transparent performance evaluation process open to representatives of private sector, consumer, and civil society organizations will enhance trust in the functioning of these boards.

An efficient legal infrastructure is also critical to the process. The independence of these boards does not mean they are unaccountable. While elected politicians should not meddle in the daily affairs of these boards of independent regulatory bodies, these boards should be responsible to the elected politicians for efficient functioning in-line with adopted economic policies.

The principles for efficient functioning of these boards are:

1. an effective level of knowledge;
2. transparency and participation;
3. public benefit identified as the performance criterion;
4. expedient decision making and implementation;
5. decisiveness.

Effective level of knowledge – in order to anticipate the actions of market players, comprehend them, and establish the rules to steer them to the benefit of the public requires a high level of technical, economic, systemic knowledge and skill. Therefore a cadre of individuals specialized in different areas working together is most desirable, and this requires adequate compensation and reward systems for managing these boards.

Transparency and participation – the effectiveness of these boards is highly dependent on the trust of market players and society at large. To earn this trust, it is not sufficient that the board has high levels of capability. Decisions taken behind closed doors have an adverse impact on trust. The processes of these boards have to be transparent and be structured to take into account input from various stakeholders.

Public benefit identified as the performance criterion – during the decision making of these boards, it is important to justify how public benefit is impacted. Keeping sight of public benefit ensures consistency since it also entails fairness and sharing with the public.

Expedient decision making and implementation – delayed justice is injustice. If the board lags behind in adjusting to changing conditions or market developments, or making decisions, then market players lose their confidence in the arbitration of the board. Therefore, transparency and participation should be accompanied by expedient decision making and implementation.

Decisiveness – there should be clear punitive measures for noncompliance, and examples should be easily understood by the public. It is important for the boards to have enough autonomy to be able to move against large or powerful players.

Autonomy is a fine balance. It should not be deemed as authority without accountability by the boards. The responsibility is ultimately with the political authority, which determines the "public benefit," economic policies, and targets. Responsibility for formulation of policy rests with elected representatives, and responsibility for implementation through appropriate processes rests with regulatory boards.

Autonomy of the regulatory agencies should be perceived not as policy making in place of the elected representatives, but to implement the policies they make without any concessions to political pressures or lobbyists.

FINANCING OLD AGE

Even though demographic developments can be easily projected, they are not sufficiently used in future planning. Advancements in medical science, fewer large-scale wars, general economic growth despite skewed income distribution, urbanization leading to smaller families are all leading to an ageing population. Social security systems that are based on the working population meeting the cost of retired population are becoming more and more inadequate as the proportion of retired population to working population increases. Moreover, the higher cost of healthcare and lengthening old age, which requires more healthcare, has the effect of increasing deficits not only through social security payments but also higher healthcare costs.

When financing these deficits becomes untenable, relationships between generations may be strained, and prioritizing among the old population for healthcare may be necessary, leading to tensions and chaos. These possibilities require careful future planning.

Increasing the retirement age and taking steps to employ people productively for longer periods should take priority in planning not only legislative measures, but should also be taken into account in company policies. People who live longer and in better health should also be able to work and produce longer. This calls for a renewed perspective on life.

Achieving sustainable economic growth is the key to addressing these issues. This requires a focus on the education of future generations. Well-educated entrepreneurs and a well educated labor force are the cornerstones of sound economic development.

DIGITAL TECHNOLOGY: THE NEW INDUSTRIAL REVOLUTION

The Internet Revolution has removed barriers of time and place in communication, enabled access to information at low cost, and enriched the sharing of information. This information technology is revolutionary because it not only accelerates development of science and innovation, but also forces cultural and social transformation.

The speed with which information can be processed also enables interdisciplinary integration thereby speeding up development and creation of knowledge. The increase in wealth brought about by the mass production during the Industrial Revolution is now being redefined with information sharing over the Internet. As with every revolution, there will be winners and losers. However, there is no doubt that the winners will be the leaders in grasping this transformation. This is as true for countries as it is for individuals, companies, and institutions.

E-GOVERNMENT

The basic question is how to take advantage of the opportunities presented by the technological revolution, and the summary answer points to a high level of responsibility for politicians. To be a leading "digital state," the state has to:

- enable the infrastructure for access both in terms of technology and appropriate pricing mechanisms;
- structure public services delivery through the Internet thereby providing cheap, efficient, and timely service;
- enable NGOs and individuals to participate in policy formulation processes by using new means of communication;
- enact facilitating legal arrangements such as digital signature, and
- educate its citizens in adapting successfully to a digital economy.

On the one hand, individuals are raising their expectations from companies or the state as a consumer of their products and services, and on the other, they are being expected to perform more as entrepreneurs or employees. The digital economy is transforming all segments, and the state is not exempt.

Therefore e-state projects are enjoying a high level of political support across the world. Governments are placing priority emphasis on investment in technology and e-state projects. The most efficient way to improve the quality of life for its stakeholders is to improve management quality in it institutions, systems, and to adopt good governance principles.

GOOD GOVERNANCE IN THE PUBLIC SECTOR: TESEV EXPERIENCE IN TURKIYE

In order to increase their effectiveness of the public sector, public authorities should adopt a participative attitude in designing regulatory functions. They should benefit from the market mechanisms in their areas of service provision and they should include the voices of citizens in determining the priorities of public service.

Turkiye is in the process of implementing structural reforms in public sector. Within this context, TESEV (Türkiye Ekonomik ve Sosyal Etüdler Vakfı [Turkish Economic and Social Studies Foundation]), a leading think-tank in Turkiye, aims to: (a) improve the quality of the strategic planning processes of local governments for the realizations of subsidiarity and effectiveness principles; (b) help establish organizations and processes for increasing participation; and (c) create methods to increase accessibility to information necessary for ensuring meaningful participation with the principles of transparency, accountability, and consistency and enabling the systematization of information to provide input to public decision making.

In line with these goals TESEV embarked on a project called "Good Governance: Improving Quality of Life: Building Civil Society Capacity for Effective Local Service Delivery." This project was financed by a grant provided by the Japan Social Development Fund through the World Bank. The project that started in May 2005 and ended in April 2008 had the objective of developing citizen participation in the decision-making mechanisms in order to improve the efficiency and effectiveness of the utilization of public resources in Turkiye.

The "Good Governance: Improving Quality of Living" project aims to realize good governance and to use public resources in a participative manner and according to strategic plans. It aims to develop tools that are tried in pilot projects and to improve good governance experience in Turkiye.

The objective has been to develop institutional capacity building through collaboration of civil society and universities. A further objective has been to build experience for stakeholders by designing strategic plans with the collaboration of civil society, mayors, and governors.

Maybe the most innovative aspect of this project has been the tools developed for the presentation of inputs that are crucial to the governance process. Socio-Economic Development Maps, Public Expenditure Analysis, and Public Service Satisfaction Surveys are examples of this. Crucial regular Impact Analysis reports identified the extent to which these strategic plans are put into use and to judge performance by comparing with best-practice cases.

If public policy formulation processes are not based on knowledge, effective utilization of public resources would be a rare event. Yet, prior to the Good Governance project, in Turkiye most of the decisions such as the positioning of dispensaries or homes for elderly people were made without a consideration of the location of the users (Socio-Economic Development Maps were not used). Since spending decisions were made through various channels through an unconsolidated manner, the effectiveness of these resources was not properly evaluated (Public Expenditure Analyses were not made). Since, the preferences of citizens were not taken into account, effective use of public services was not guaranteed (Public Service Satisfaction Surveys were not used).

Further, whenever information input to public policy formulation was not presented in comparison to best practices or such information was not easily accessible neither the participation of civil society, nor learning from best practices took place. For this reason, mapping of information, the establishment of a common database where different public authorities can easily monitor the expenditures made for the same end users, the development of analytical abilities, and the promotion of learning from best practices will enhance the quality of public decision making.

There are certain preconditions for increasing participation, which is the basis of good governance. They are:

1. the creation of processes open to participation;
2. bringing together the civil society organizations that will ensure effective participation;
3. ensuring that participants have access to information and that necessary training for meaningful participation is provided.

For the implementation of this project, six pilot provinces were selected from different parts of the country. The aim of the project was to improve the quality of strategic planning processes of local governments by applying subsidiarity and effectiveness principles and to strengthen the local civil society organizations in the following ways:

1. to create a dialogue between local civil society organizations and local political authorities;
2. to equip local actors with tools for analytically monitoring and auditing local policy decisions;
3. to increase the participation of local civil society organizations and universities in decision-making, especially planning and budgeting processes;
4. to create methods to increase accessibility to information necessary for ensuring meaningful participation;
5. to focus on education, health, infrastructure and elimination of poverty and to diversify and increase the quality of local services, systemizing information to provide input to public decision making.

The "Good Governance – Improving Quality of Life" project developed tools that local governments can utilize during the strategic planning, the monitoring of results and the evaluation stages. The widespread use of the tools developed in this project serves both to strengthen the current public sector reform and to ensure the use of public resources in a way that will maximize citizen satisfaction.

Information is necessary for the improvement in the quality of decisions. For this reason, three main studies are carried out within the scope of the project:

A. socio-economic development maps;
B. public expenditure analyses;
C. public service satisfaction surveys.

All three tools provide critical inputs to form the basis of participatory strategic planning.

The *Socio-Economic Development Maps* were calculated for every level of administration from the neighborhoods to provincial level, with an index that is composed of six indices and 76 variables. Since socio-economic development maps visually depict the variation in development and expenditure levels, they provide invaluable guidance to local civic actors and local decision-makers in terms of setting priorities and designing appropriate policies.

In this manner, information obtained at the end of these studies is easily understood by the citizens. Hence the decisions in strategic plans about which services and which areas should be given priority are based on sound evidence that is easily shared with all participants in the decision processes.

Nonetheless, in order to claim that the really needy have access to public services, it is mandatory that we know how public money is being spent. *Public Expenditure Analyses* have been developed for citizens to keep track of public spending patterns on a provincial and district level. They can monitor how much and to which functions the public money is being directed. In this way, they can create pressure mechanisms on local authorities about their budgetary decisions.

Citizen Satisfaction Surveys aim to measure the satisfaction of citizens about the local services help local policy makers discover the impact of their policies, the expectations of residents, and possible ways of ameliorating their services.

These tools together prove useful as they are utilized systematically and over an extended period of time and also as they are used by local civic actors while formulating their demands.

In developing and utilizing these tools, it became apparent that many public officials were not aware of the total public expenditures and their distribution in their province by beneficiary and by development area.

This was due to the fact that along with the budgets of the special provincial administration and the municipality, public resources are transferred through very different channels such as health card payments for the needy, scholarships provided by the central government, social security payments, with no coordination or consolidation of results. Therefore, it became clear that public expenditures were not analyzed or reviewed by their results or by their beneficiaries, rendering it impossible to improve their effectiveness.

Presentation of the information in a **comparative method** is a tool to ensure **continuous assessment**. In this way, the differences in effectiveness observed among provinces and neighborhoods concerning important issues such as education, health, and security are opened to discussion by the citizens and hence, effectiveness of public resources could be increased through learning and in-line with priorities. In this context, the right to access information is an important tool that will facilitate the supervision of the implementation of strategic plans by the public.

If secondary legislation (i.e., declaration, statute, regulation) is prepared with the participation of civil society organizations rather than by the bureaucracy unilaterally, effectiveness of implementation is significantly enhanced. Therefore, policies developed for legislation ideally need to be shared with the public at the draft stage. This should ensure that a sufficient level of opinion exchange takes place. The public need to voice their opinion transparently on appropriate platforms where different opinions can be voiced. On these platforms, decisions need to be supported by a rational approach and on the basis of scientifically performed research. That is why one of the most important factors that determine the effectiveness of civil society organizations is the preparation of scientific studies to provide input to the process of policy formulation.

To be effective and fair, implementation should take place after a transitional period that is sufficient for relevant parties to adapt themselves without risking realization of the policy. Expecting small local administrations that are already grappling with funds management to take on and deal with more responsibility and to manage larger sums of public money effectively would probably be unproductive.

The participatory approach required by good governance can become effective and efficient in the societal sense only through the adoption of a "national education" system that is accessible to all, focuses on the rights and responsibilities of citizens, and actively encourages the citizens to participate in decisions that influence their lives.

As it is highly difficult for every citizen to participate in every decision making process directly, it is important that well-functioning civil society organizations are developed in these provinces and that their management capacities are developed so that they are able to be the agents of participation.

However, civil society organizations are not sufficient to ensure participation. There are two more requirements for the decisions to be taken in a participatory manner:

1. Officials that use public authority in the provinces, such as the governor and mayor, should encourage participation by demonstrating a management approach open to participation.
2. The process of collaboration of the representatives of civil society organizations with the elected or appointed managers authorized to take the final decisions with regards to funds utilization should be clearly formulated.

The "Good Governance: Improving Quality of Life" project of TESEV aimed to create best practice examples that will be able to form the basis of improving transparency and accountability by supporting the participation of the public to government and consequently, to achieve a better response to citizens' needs. Therefore good governance is the main methodology to improve the quality of the decisions taken and therefore to improve the quality of life through more effective use of public resources.

The widespread use of the tools developed in this project will both strengthen current public sector reform and will ensure the use of public resources in a way that will maximize citizen satisfaction. Obviously, these tools are open to further development. It should be emphasized that the fact that these tools were used for the first time as input for public decision making and local strategic plans is quite innovative in itself. With the widespread use of these tools, public resources will be utilized not according to the priorities of influential and politically powerful groups, but according to sensible information that ensures access to public services for the poor and the minimization of the developmental gap between regions.

In short, good governance is the most effective tool for improving the quality of life in a country.

PUBLIC SECTOR REFORM IN TURKIYE

An effective state is fundamental in order for citizens to have opportunities to enhance their welfare and live as a community.

According to surveys a significant portion of the citizens in Turkiye are unhappy with the public administration. In a famous speech, Martin Luther King said: "What protects the society are those people who have positive expectations from their country. The most dangerous of all projects would be to design a society where people have no hopes whatsoever from the place they live in."

One of the areas citizens complain about the most is corruption in the public sector. Another equally problematic area is the wastefulness due to populism. According to a study carried out by the State Planning Organization, the projected completion period for public works projects was three-and-a-half to five-and-a-half years. In practice however, these projects were completed between 9 and 15 years.

This shows that we should fight not only corruption, but also inefficiency. It would be ideal to have a university or an airport in each province. However, if we do not spend public resources in a needs-based way, it will be impossible to realize the projected benefits of any projects.

It would be costly to try to delay change in our country. It is fundamental that we try to focus on the institutions as well as the people working in those institutions. The public sector system has major deficiencies.

First of all, the public sector is based on controlling and monitoring rather than results. According to Total Quality Management (TQM), what makes it necessary to check quality is the failings of the system. What is fundamental for TQM is to produce rather than control quality. When quality is controlled we are still stuck with its costs, whereas when high quality public services are provided, efficiency is achieved.

When looked at from this angle, it is easy to see that the public system does not trust its employees. Therefore it does not authorize them to exercise judgment. The case of the Public Procurement Law provides an example. According to this law, it is compulsory to reward the bidder with the lowest price offer, generally without sufficient assurance of minimum quality. Even in our private decisions, we all prefer to get the best price but not necessarily the cheapest goods. To the contrary, provided that it is within our budget limits, we seek the highest value and quality, rather than the cheapest supply. Why should the public sector not be managed in that fashion?

A further example is that of central administration. Everything is managed from the centre since there is a lack of trust in local authorities. How much success can be achieved with this kind of attitude? Another example is personnel policies. Every employee is given the same salary since we do not believe that managers will make their decisions on the basis of employees' merit. Therefore success is not rewarded – Further more such policies promote laziness and hinder initiative taking in the public sector.

Another consideration is that the Turkish state system is based on measuring the inputs rather than the outputs. For instance, the success of the Ministry of Energy should be based not on how much investment is made but on the availability and price competitiveness of electricity compared with other countries. The success of our Telecom system should be understood not from how much privatization revenue has been generated but from how economic and widespread the telecommunication service is.

Another failure of the Turkish system is that we do not have a long-term perspective when designing public policies. Since the Government does not have multiyear budgets, projects take longer to complete than originally projected. The system is prone to wastefulness as it does not have an accrual-based budget.

By decreasing the flexibility of the budget items and by not admitting the unused portion of these items as savings for the next budget term, wastefulness at the end of each fiscal year is promoted. Is there a point in preventing successful managers who want to carry their savings to the next budget term?

In order to prevent corruption and achieve continuous progress, accountability, transparency, consistency, and effectiveness are crucial. What is the drawback of external auditing of all public functions? What is the use of limiting citizens' access to how the public resources are utilized with the pretext of state secret or financial secret? What is the gain in evading accountability for the services provided to citizens?

We have to prioritize the following principles in realizing the public sector reform:

1. Public administration should be transparent both within and to the public.
2. Public administration should be held accountable for the way it uses public authority and resources.
3. Public policies should be designed in a way to maximize public good.
4. Public resources should be used in a way that will not jeopardize fiscal discipline and should be used in an efficient manner.
5. Merit and knowledge rather than political loyalties should be the basis upon which public appointments are made.

In order to gain citizens' confidence in public management it is crucial to put thriftiness, efficiency, and effectiveness into action.

Thriftiness means the prevention of wasteful spending of public resources. It is against the principle of thriftiness if resources are used for investments that will never pay back, or if employment is created for factories that will never function.

Efficiency requires the production of more goods and services with less capital and labor, resulting in lower unit costs. The public budget is a third of Turkiye's GDP. This does not include the total value of land, buildings, and equipment owned by the public authorities. It is not a new fact that there is a great potential for efficiency gains in the public sector.

However, the most important concept within all these is effectiveness. To be effective is to have outputs that are the most significant and beneficial for the citizens. If a service you produce efficiently is of no use to anyone, it means the resources are wasted. For instance, it is of trivial importance that a road has been built in the most efficient manner, if it is not utilized.

It is important to be aware of the great individual, institutional, and societal impediments to the achievement of effectiveness. In order to be able to use public resources effectively, the management capacity, the motivation, and the knowledge base of the public sector should be improved fundamentally.

In order to sustain this progress, we need to institutionalize participation, transparency, accountability, and performance-based management in our public administration. We have to abandon the habit of controlling only the inputs and move to systems that are based on also monitoring the outputs.

For the culture of accountability to take root in Turkiye, the figures that are appointed to leading political and bureaucratic positions should free themselves of the image of "the sovereign." Unchecked spending powers of public figures should be replaced with a system based on responsible management of public resources. It is crucial to invest in the communication of the accountability concept in order to realize these stated objectives.

A further method of employing an effective performance-based system is to create a human resources policy that is open both to reward and punishment. The most important of all though, is the prevalence of merit-based human resource policies rather than personnel policies designed to reward political loyalties.

Promoting participation, consistency, and transparency is crucial in gaining citizens' support in public policies. This is the only way for public policies to be citizen-focused and effective.

The concept of policy development is confused with the concept of politics. In fact, generally political decisions are usually not based on scientific assessments that consider the impact of the decision. Due to this deficiency, either it becomes impossible to disentangle certain results from various political decisions or citizen confidence is eroded due to frequent changes and amendments made to previous decisions.

For instance, in many developed countries the process of making tax policy includes: (1) an institutional mechanism that embraces the participation of tax payers, (2) the economic modeling of the impact of the tax policy before and after its ratification, and (3) a transparent and accountable process of law making. In Turkiye, however, tax policies are designed behind closed doors without the full and transparent assessment of their economic impact and with the sole objective of maximizing revenues. Due to this, sectors slide to informal economic activity or lose their global competitiveness.

The reason why scientific contributions to policy-making processes is minuscule is not only because politicians are insensitive, but also because there are not sufficient resources for policy studies and that scientists are not very interested in public policy related research. Yet, the social cost of a badly designed public policy can be enormous. Hence, it is to the benefit of the public that we devote more resources to think-tanks in Turkiye.

An additional problem is that public authorities are not utilizing existing public policy research. There are various reasons: (1) researchers do not deal with real-world problems or their work is not result oriented, (2) the results of studies are not easily available or there are not enough resources for the results to be communicated to relevant authorities, and (3) politicians misunderstand study results or researchers do not effectively communicate their research and conclusions.

It is of utmost importance that politicians, bureaucrats, and researchers create effective communication channels from the initial stages of the research so that these studies can become result oriented and effective tools in public policy making.

To be able to effectively communicate research results, it is crucial that the study is written in a language accessible to the target group and that a successful public relations campaign is implemented to publicize the results. Another consideration is to communicate research results in a way that will be interesting to different target groups without sacrificing academic honesty.

In order to make research results easily understood it may be necessary to devote resources to the education of bureaucrats and politicians to enable them to consciously use the results. It would also be useful if researchers were encouraged to communicate their work in a language that is accessible to those who are not academics, but who are end users or beneficiaries.

One of the most important factors that affect the administrative success in a country is the quality of its policies and the effectiveness of their implementation. Making use of scientific research will surely enhance the management quality in Turkiye.

Hence we could summarize the approach that is needed in public policy development as the following:

In policy making:

1. Any public policy should enhance the welfare of the end user (the public.) For instance, the EU Consumer Policy text contains the statement the "EU takes all its decisions to enhance consumer welfare."
2. Policies should not favor certain parties to the detriment of others.
3. Policies should be transparently shared with the public (open declaration).

In policy implementation:

1. Public policy decisions should be focused on the main goals, priorities, and results and should be supported by flexible implementation regulation.
2. The legislation should be shared with the public as a draft law. For this purpose:
    a. Draft laws should be based on potential impact analyses, preferably by multiple sources.
    b. The draft law should be declared in an attempt to create a public forum for the relevant stakeholders. The stakeholders should be able to voice their position in relevant ways according to their interests.
    c. The amendments made after further consultation should not be based on which stakeholder is more influential, but according to evidence based on rational assessments.
3. The legislation should become effective after a transition period that is long enough to accommodate the adjustment of relevant stakeholders, but short enough that will avoid any delays and that will guarantee the successful implementation of the policy.

A system that makes policies more understandable and implementation more effective and is based on consensus should be created. This should include:

1. Policies that are developed in an open, transparent, understandable, and concrete manner, in a way that takes into account the views of all parties and that is based on individual rights and liberties.

2. Policies that are declared through all public channels and not through certain cliques.
3. Policies that are not window dressing for a hidden agenda.
4. Policy developers who are open to democratic consultations and who are courageous enough to promote long-term community interests rather than falling prey to short-term populist policies, in spite of public pressures. The reason is, that one objective of successful public policies is to guarantee the welfare and rights of future generations. For this reason, it is important to be courageous and resist populist urges.
5. The legalization of legislation through primary laws that are solely legislative in nature not through mechanisms such as the decree with the force of law, since it confuses legislative and executive powers. (Decree with the Force of Law is against the principle of separation of powers since it replaces the legislative power with the executive power.) The Primary laws should state not what should be done, but rather what should not be done.
6. Have primary laws that describe what the policy in question is, rather than how it is going to be carried out.
7. State how the policies are to be carried out and be clarified with secondary legislation (such as bylaws). This secondary legislation should be produced through the collaboration of bureaucracy and civil society. The preparation of the secondary legislation solely by the bureaucracy without consulting the public opinion will jeopardize the effectiveness of its implementation.
8. Design participative mechanisms for the election of the managers responsible for the implementation of public policies. This is crucial. For instance, in appointing the members and the heads of regulatory bodies, merit instead of political loyalty should be decisive. The determination of the qualifications of a suitable candidate is more important than from which institution that candidate comes. The potential of candidates to form an effective team should also be considered before appointments are made. These appraisals and appointments should be made in a way that will include a transparent consultation with civil society and market actors. Broadcasting this procedure through a public TV channel will increase public confidence in these institutions.
9. Guarantee the effectiveness of public institutions, through clear performance criteria. The performance criteria should be based on benchmarks, preferably from other countries. For instance, the Energy Market Regulatory Board should make the attainment of

competitive energy prices, the provision of energy in every place where there is demand in the cheapest way possible, a primary objective. Making performance results available for discussion in the private sector and civil society will enhance the trust of citizens in the state. To this end, regulatory impact analysis should be made regularly and shared with the public in an open manner.

10. Not forget that an efficient and timely judicial system is crucial for the healthy functioning of public institutions. It is crucial that performance results are discussed in a transparent, result oriented manner even if at a fundamental level public institutions are only responsible to judicial authorities.

In societies where public policy makers and those that are affected by policies do not communicate, public sector management falls under the influence of those who are political allies of the ruling elites. The collaboration of policy makers and citizens is the best way to achieve a sustainable social accord.

As a result, public sector reform should not only be seen as a legislative process, but also as a cultural change. Resources should be devoted to the education of society and public authorities and for intense campaigning in order for this cultural transformation to take place.

CHAPTER 5

Civil Society for Good Governance

Meaning in life is making meaningful contributions to others.

'Real generosity to the future lies in giving all to the present.' (Albert Camus).

Under changing global conditions, the relationship between citizens and their public administrations are undergoing a transformation, as are definitions of concepts such as democracy and human rights. Individuals' participation in local or global decision making processes to shape their own future is emerging as the primary concern. Such participation forms the basis for redefining the concepts of democracy and human rights.

FROM RULING TO GOVERNANCE

As the relationship between individuals and their public administrations is being restructured in today's world, the concept of "ruling" is also going through a transformation, to be replaced by the concept of "governance."

Success in public policy making would be increasingly difficult if this transformation remains unnoticed. It is important to note the change because civil society organizations are instrumental in shaping the standards, in the gathering and dissemination of the information that feeds decision making, and problem solving, and more importantly in realizing participatory democracy. Nevertheless, it should not be overlooked that the role of civil society organizations is not to take the place of the elected or public organizations, but to challenge them in order to support and improve their functioning in a participatory manner.

Institutions in pursuit of constantly improving management quality have been instrumental in creating the concept of good governance. Civil society organizations are the most effective instruments of change in the transition from ruling to governance.

CIVIL SOCIETY ORGANIZATIONS FOR GOOD GOVERNANCE

Over time, the concept of democracy has turned to "representative" from "participatory" as both the number of participants, and the complexity and diversity of the decisions has increased. However, the interests of the representatives do not necessarily always match societal interests, and as the desire of individuals to participate in decisions influencing their lives has increased, with technological developments in education and communication, the concept has further evolved in the twenty-first century and a new form of participatory democracy has emerged: civil society organizations have started to formulate societal decisions in cooperation with the elected bodies. Overlooking the significance of this transformation would make public policy making increasingly difficult.

An increasing number of people believe that the twenty-first century will be marked by the impact of civil society organizations. Subscribers to this view point out that only such organizations have the ability to effectively mobilize the potential of the community at large.

This is true largely because the inherent need in human nature "to be useful," to follow a purpose without financial compensation, and to add value to the community can be most effectively satisfied through involvement in civil society organizations. These organizations can successfully cultivate and direct the constructive and creative potential of large numbers of people to specific purposes for the benefit of society.

Civil society organizations have been instrumental in mobilizing human and financial resources for a wide variety of global issues from the environment to health to education to rights for the disabled where government resources alone are insufficient to solve problems.

NGOs have raised the specter for awareness of environmental issues, leading to civil movements that were eventually instrumental in big oil companies reconsidering some of their positions. Some other important initiatives developed by NGOs are the antislavery movement, and the International Campaign to Ban Land Mines.

Good governance takes place at four levels in society: (1) public level, (2) private sector level, (3) NGO level, and (4) individual level.

Good governance at the public level depends on the ability of state organizations and public service organizations to encourage participation. It also depends on a consistent, transparent, and accountable public administration that ensures the fairness and effectiveness of decisions and their implementation. The cure for almost all problems that we face in society such as corruption, inefficiency, and improvidence is to fully adopt and implement the principles of good governance. Civil society organizations may assume a very important role in such a process. By cooperating with specialized civil society organizations, the state would be able to deal with national issues in a manner that enhances the trust in its institutions.

Second, at the private sector level good governance may be realized through two interlinked channels. On the one hand, corporations themselves apply corporate governance and in line with that they implement transparency, accountability, a participatory form of management, and effectiveness and efficiency in their own management structures. On the other hand, by allocating resources to social responsibility projects, they encourage their personnel to donate a part of their time to civil society organizations in voluntary projects. The Corporate Volunteers Association, which has been established by some of the leading corporations in this field, provides support for the development of social responsibility in Turkiye.

Third, when the civil society organizations apply good governance principles in their own operations; the principles of "Total Quality Management," and choose both their own personnel and recipients of their services based on merit-based processes, they become both more effective and provide benchmark examples for good governance principle. Civil society organizations that participate in public sector decision-making mechanisms through the Local Agenda 21 play a leading role in this field.

Finally, individuals carry an important responsibility in the realization of good governance principles. At the personal level, every human being is a consumer, a citizen, and also an individual with social responsibilities. Adopting good governance principles such as consistency, responsibility, accountability, fairness, transparency, participation, and effectiveness while fulfilling these responsibilities will contribute to the development of all types of institutions – including civil society organizations – and to increasing social welfare. This should ensure that a more effective utilization of the limited resources will be achieved. Therefore, each of us as an individual should demand good governance from the state, from companies and from civil society organizations while at the same time trying to become model individuals practicing these principles. We should not forget that the solution starts from within.

There are certain preconditions for increasing participation that are the basis of good governance: (i) the creation of processes open to participation, (ii) bringing together the civil society organizations to ensure effective participation, and (iii) making sure that participants have access to information and that necessary training for meaningful participation is provided.

However, NGOs are vital in improving the participation of companies and individuals into governance mechanisms to improve the quality of governance.

SOCIAL ENTREPRENEURSHIP REQUIRES COMPREHENSIVE PLANNING

NGOs have to act like "social entrepreneurs" in order to be able to fulfill good governance principles. Some common criteria that social entrepreneurs have to observe when undertaking projects to address social issues can be summarized as follows:

1. the project should address a tangible need;
2. the project should be managed by an effective team;
3. the project should lend itself to replication if successfully completed;
4. the project should have sufficient funding in order to meet its ongoing expenses;
5. the project results and benefits should be regularly measured and shared.

Unfortunately many NGOs are satisfied with having the goal of "doing good" rather than focusing on innovation and entrepreneurship that in itself has great potential to make a difference and "do good." More recently new organizational forms that represent an intersection of an NGO and a for-profit venture that feature social entrepreneurship are evolving. One of the key examples of this new form of organization is the Grameen Bank, its main focus is to provide the poor with access to credit to empower them, but at the same time makes a profit.

SOCIAL ENTERPRISES REQUIRE EFFECTIVENESS TOO

Another important concept to observe is "effectiveness." Until recently, effectiveness was considered solely as a commercial term. Concepts such as "goodwill" and "altruism" were only applicable to social projects. It has now become clear that productivity is not only a commercial concept, but one that has to be taken into account by all institutions that intend to achieve.

Good governance, creativity, and innovation are as critical to NGOs as they are to business enterprises. NGOs rely largely on volunteers to achieve their aims, and hence have no available means to enforce the effectiveness of their members other than their persuasive ability to rally them around a cause. This feature is both a strength and a weakness.

While NGOs have only recently been emerging as influential actors in the international decision making arena, their role will be increasingly important in this millennium. The successful political leaders of the era will also be those who are able to put this development in context and take the growing influence of NGOs into account.

Civil society organizations are instrumental in shaping the standards, in the gathering and dissemination of the information that feeds decision making and problem solving, and hence in both facilitating and enforcing practice of participatory democracy. If states cooperate with specialized NGOs in resolving issues, they stand to identify solutions that inspire more trust in their citizens, as well as promoting participatory democracy.

In Turkiye, the Turkish Industrialists and Businessmen Association (TUSIAD) and the Turkish Economic and Social Studies Foundation (TESEV) are two examples of well organized NGOs that support legislative process by providing information and research support. Several other NGOs have given significant support to Turkiye's development process.

GOOD GOVERNANCE RECOMMENDATIONS FOR NGOs

There is a simple yet effective management style that can help more NGOs make a difference. Since NGOs are not directly responsible to any formal bodies, there are some critical aspects of their management.

NGOs should clearly define their mission and vision in a participatory manner, and share these widely. The mission and the vision must address a concrete need within the community, must be open to participation by people sensitive to the issue, and should define targets that are reachable and compelling. In order to realize change, there must be a clear vision of what will be achieved as a result of the NGO activity. For example, targeting an improvement in the standards of education within a specific geographical area is not the same as targeting an improvement in the standards of education nationwide. Organizational approach, resource requirements, and the organizations and area to be included would be different in each case.

MOBILIZING RESOURCES AND COALITIONS

NGOs should be able to establish a strategy for resource development that is compatible with the vision. Resources go beyond just financial ones. Human and information resources are just as important when

---

carrying out change. Identifying and mobilizing relevantly experienced people as well as people that have the ability to reach and establish effective communication with various segments of society are important in order to establish wide support for the project and to bring about change. It is necessary to have a small and effective NGO professional team to maintain focus, motivation and to keep projects moving forward. A knowledgeable and seasoned core professional team is highly instrumental in employing a volunteer force productively.

In order to be able to use the resources of others, NGOs need to build coalitions with other capable parties that are sympathetic to their mission. Social change can only happen with comprehensive planning and execution. Since performance improvement needs to be measured, performance criteria should be established and project developments measured against the criteria.

Creative solutions and initiative taking should be encouraged to arrive at desired outcomes and future leaders should be trained in the process. Creating an environment conducive to information sharing and participation is essential to disseminating the message of the NGO and making a difference in the community.

CRITICAL ASPECTS IN PRACTICE: COOPERATION, FOCUS, RESOURCE MANAGEMENT, AND COMMUNICATION

Three factors are critical for success: (i) it is the mission and not the NGO itself that is important, therefore sharing and cooperation should be emphasized; (ii) all resources should be focused on the mission and not be distracted to other activities simply in order to raise the profile; and (iii) effectiveness of resource utilization and the resulting social impact has to be continuously monitored to ensure sustainability.

Communication is an important element that should be taken into consideration when planning resource utilization. Considering that NGOs have no sanctioning abilities, their only weapon is their power of persuasion. To use this weapon effectively requires concentrated communication with relevant parties. Establishing parallels between the agenda of the community and the mission of the NGO and using these in communication can facilitate support for the mission.

NGOs have limited resources and are constantly seeking ways to increase these resources. Constituting an institutional identity and prioritizing effective communication are essential to gain access to further resources. Accomplishments are the most effective vehicles of communication. Therefore, successful examples of activity in keeping with the NGO's mission should be created, repeated, and their success widely disseminated. For example, effective results obtained by the Turkish Search and Rescue Organization (AKUT) during the 1999 earthquake in Turkiye has increased their credibility and resources within the country, and has also promoted them in the international scene. As a result AKUT was able make significant contributions during the aftermath of the major Indian and Iranian earthquakes in 2001 and 2003, respectively.

Good NGO leadership is another critical success factor. Social leadership requires clear definition of goals, principles, and values for social responsibility, communicating these within and outside the organization, and demonstrating ownership of these goals, principles, and values by actions. The working relationship principles adopted to achieve the NGO's mission should overlap with good governance principles. Sustainability of its activity is only possible if the NGO inspires confidence in the community.

Good governance principles should be relentlessly applied within the NGO. An NGO should be improving its activities constantly with respect to the consistency, responsibility, accountability, fairness, transparency, and effectiveness principles of good governance and closely examine its deployment in the organization. NGOs should actively exhibit transparency both within the organization and vis-à-vis their supporters about the utilization of their resources.

NGOs that subscribe to good governance principles and choose their managers on the basis of merit rather than favoritism establish not only efficient governance of their own organization but also serve as examples for good governance that become widespread and take root. In this context, it is important to note the joint activity of KalDer, the Turkish Quality Association, and Bogazici University, to establish a management certificate program to train future NGO professionals to improve the effectiveness of NGOs.

TRAINING, INNOVATION, AND INSTITUTION BUILDING

Change can only be achieved by education. Training programs and developing case studies are instrumental in NGOs achieving their mission. Conducting or commissioning research, and gathering and sharing effective relevant statistics are important tools of change.

Last but not least, regardless of how important a good leader is, there is a need for institution building within the NGO as well. Both the board and the professional staff should be well prepared for turnover and succession planning.

Just as in the business world, innovation, creativity, and good management are crucial to volunteer organizations that wish to effect societal change.

STANDARD BEARER FOR TOTAL QUALITY: THE KalDer CASE

To earn international recognition and command respect, Turkiye needs to be in a position to contribute to the solutions of global problems. This is not possible through foreign relations on government level alone. NGO involvement is a necessary complement. In trade, commerce, science, culture, arts, and technology international relationships have assumed a civil identity. KalDer (Turkish Quality Association) is a leading NGO in developing and spreading the management quality concept, and deserves special mention to illustrate how it applies the principles identified here.

KalDer has defined as its mission the motivation and preparation of an appropriate environment for all organizations public, private or non-profit-making, in which these organizations attain world-class quality level and increase their competitiveness. On the one hand, it is working to become an exemplary organization in the world through efficient deployment and use of the Total Quality Management (TQM) throughout Turkiye, and on the other, it operates as an example of an NGO practicing good governance principles within its organization.

KalDer's mission and vision have been defined in a participatory manner. Its success is determined by consistent focus of all activities toward the identified goal. This focus has put Turkiye on the map as one of the countries in Europe with the most European Foundation for Quality Management (EFQM) award winning companies. It has also successfully given depth and breadth to the concept of quality, creating examples all over Turkiye with diverse organizations and companies, large or small. It has also secured participation of public institutions such as the Ministry of Education, the Ministry of Labor, and the Under Secretariat of Customs in the civil initiative National Quality Movement (NQM).

As a first in the world, KalDer has introduced a separate quality award for NGOs, and encouraged the practice of TQM by NGOs by providing training. All this has been made possible by its unwavering focus.

THE NOVELTY OF KalDer MANAGEMENT

KalDer has structured its organization in line with its mission and vision. The solidity of its management structure has been made possible through the practice of the "manager on loan," where institutions that support KalDer lend one of their managers experienced in total quality management to KalDer for a period of two years. Candidates are identified by the KalDer board from among leaders with the potential to mobilize resources for comprehensive application of quality concept who are working for institutions that employ TQM. These managers have the skills to reach and communicate with various segments of society to effectively realize KalDer's mission and vision. The strength of management also enables efficient use of volunteer time.

KalDer places special emphasis on communications. To change behavior in people or institutions, the first challenge is to convince them of the need and benefits of the change. Therefore, KalDer has given priority to engaging professional support in establishing its institutional culture and public relations. Fully aware that successful precedents are the best form of good communication, KalDer has defined the goal of NQM as creating successful cases in different segments and ensuring the information about these cases is widely shared with the public.

KalDer also allocates resources to developing specific content from successful applications of TQM in schools, municipalities, and NGOs, supporting articles, books, or case studies to be written, developing training programs, and offering workshops.

Forming alliances and cooperation with other organizations is another important area of emphasis. One such important relationship is with TUSIAD whose member companies were the primary targets for introduction and internalization of TQM. In order to closely follow developments in Europe and ensure adoption in Turkiye, KalDer has also become a National Cooperation Partner of the European Foundation for Quality Management. Other good examples include the Quality Focus cooperation protocols signed with various chambers of industry, arrangements entered into at ministry level for "training the trainers" at various public institutions, and the management certificate program for NGO managers developed with Bogazici University.

GOOD GOVERNANCE IN KalDer

KalDer actively promotes good governance concepts and ensures it adheres to good governance principles, constantly evaluating and developing its institutional behavior. Its accounts are audited by an international audit firm to support transparency of its utilization of funds. Accountability is maintained through annual reports distributed to all stakeholders and individual meetings with primary supporters. Member meetings, advisory board meetings, general assembly, specialty groups, committees, and polls are employed to ensure wide participation in effective functioning.

Institution building is given special emphasis in KalDer. A structured turnover is adopted to maintain sustainable development and creativity. Part of the institutional culture, the turnover understanding stipulates that one third of the board is renewed every term. In this way, continuity is ensured, while the board is supported and revitalized with new ideas and perspectives. Reliance on particular persons is avoided and soundness of management maintained.

PRINCIPLES OF EFFECTIVE COOPERATION WITH NGOs

There are some principles to be observed for successful cooperation between companies and NGOs:

- First and foremost there should be agreement on the purpose of cooperation and its intended achievements.
- Second, goals should be identified and measurements planned.
- Third, communication regarding the cooperation should be planned, and it must be remembered that the target audience includes parties that relate to both institutions and their collaborators.
- Finally, the efficiency of the cooperation in adding value should be monitored, and the process should constantly be open to improvement.

When providing added social value, a focused approach and efficient cooperation yield faster results, just as in business life. Favorable results add value not only to the community but also to the companies that exhibit social responsibility. Corporate support of NGOs through information and management know-how over and above financial contributions will have a significant bearing on development of the third sector, with a wider positive impact on democracy.

MANAGEMENT SUPPORT FOR NGOs

The success of associations or foundations that have made a significant social impact and gained widespread credibility can be traced to their institutional management structure. If the "manager on loan" practice, introduced by KalDer, gains broader acceptance more NGOs will have the opportunity to improve their management structure.

The "manager on loan" practice allows full-time employment in an important social cause without any adverse impact on an individual's career path. The companies that support this system use limited resources to make an important contribution to a mission they believe in. This approach also builds the leadership skills for the companies leading candidates for future promotions.

Another successful example in Turkiye of providing management support to NGOs is the Corporate Volunteers Association (CVA),[1] an NGO itself. The mission of CVA is to contribute to civil society by providing trained private sector manpower. To achieve this, CVA is aiming to spread the volunteer work concept among private sector companies and their employees and creating a dynamic relationship between community and business. CVA is also working with other NGOs in identifying social needs and developing projects to provide solutions.

By directing the human resources of its member companies, CVA promotes volunteer work, whereby both the professionals and the NGOs involved benefit from the experience. As a condition of its management support, CVA sets institutional standards for the NGOs it cooperates with, further contributing to their improved management. CVA expects these NGOs to define their mission and vision clearly, share this with their members and employees, develop projects that support their mission, open their finances to regular independent audits and share the results, apply good governance principles within their own boards, monitor performance, and carry out volunteer training programs.

CVA has three important expectations of its member companies:

1. provide information on the amount of time spent and the results of the volunteer work of their employees, and share this information publicly;
2. make volunteer work a part of their employees' performance evaluation criteria;
3. expect adherence to good governance principles at the NGOs they support, thereby promoting a sustainability of the effort to make a difference.

Engaging trained professionals in voluntary work has several benefits:

1. there can be more creative approaches to addressing social issues;
2. development of participatory democratic process is enhanced;
3. management quality of NGOs benefits from private sector experience and is improved;
4. awareness of social responsibility is raised.

A condition precedent to NGOs becoming more effective is the increased need of individuals to actively support them. This requires large numbers of people to be aware of the developments that impact their lives, to be aware they need to be informed, and to understand that they need access to various media. This is why it is critical to have access to and the ability to use information technologies. To enable this access is a global responsibility just as important as dealing with environmental issues or with the prevention of organized crime.

PRIVATE SECTOR IMPACT: THE EXAMPLE OF ARGE CONSULTING

ARGE is an Istanbul-based strategy consulting firm that also contributes significantly to improve the governance quality of numerous NGOs and activities. ARGE encourages its employees to do pro bono public work for up to one day per week and evaluates their performance on these community projects in their annual performance reviews similar to any other client project.

ARGE believes that the most important way to address the development issues is to mobilize the corporate sectors' resources for worthy causes, that is, human, innovation, technology, and business systems. Cognizant of the fact that it is a small-medium sized enterprise (SME) with 15 employees, in order to make a significant impact, ARGE aims to mobilize others' resources, in particular those of its clients, whose trust it has gained through the quality of its work.

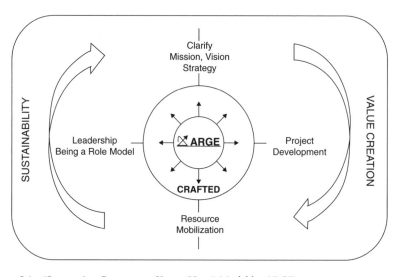

Figure 5.1 "Leveraging Governance Know–How" Model by ARGE

In order to mobilize the resources of the corporate sector for worthy causes, ARGE employs a specific **Leveraging Governance Know-how** methodology (see Figure 5.1) that has worked very effectively on various occasions, and believes the methodology is adaptable and replicable elsewhere.

ARGE Consulting employs a "Leveraging Governance Know-how" approach to mobilize and deploy resources of a broad group of companies and individuals to improve the quality of life in the community and/or country. Some of the key characteristics of this innovative approach are shown below:

1. Identify a cause to be supported and establish the reason for the support.
2. Identify companies that are likely to support this cause and mobilize some of the potential champions around the idea to establish an NGO whose sole focus will be to deliver on this cause, thereby making the cause the focal point of the collective action.
3. Make sure that the governance systems of this NGO are effective, inclusive, and do not depend on a single institution. In particular, ensure that the right people who could contribute both intellectually, as well as by mobilizing others' resources for the cause by becoming role models themselves are engaged.
4. Ensure the attraction of a small but effective team of professionals to run the day to day operations of the newly established NGO. This is critical to leverage the ideas and resources of the founders and the supporters.
5. Pay particular attention to consistency, responsibility, accountability, fairness, transparency, effectiveness of resource utilization, and deployment throughout the participating institutions (CRAFTED principles of governance). If the leaders are not role models or not trusted, it is not possible to expand the reach.
6. Develop concrete projects to be supported with specific goals and always publicly announce performance against these goals to build trust.
7. Always allocate adequate resources for internal and external communication and celebrate quick wins publicly.
8. Wherever possible, devise an award scheme to promote the right kinds of behavior for the supported cause. Make sure that there is a sound basis for the award criteria and objectivity in application of the criteria. This will ensure that the award is prestigious and attractive. The winners, in particular, have to be real role models that can stand scrutiny.

9. Make sure that the leadership of the NGO changes periodically, but that it is always a high-level executive from a role model company that assumes the leadership and becomes the spokesperson for the cause so that it is not the individuals, but the cause that gains public attention.
10. Whenever the NGO is involved in a partnership, make sure that the governance of the partners follows the CRAFTED principles.

During the past 20 years, ARGE has been instrumental in applying this methodology to establish numerous NGOs that have had significant impact in the community. In this way, ARGE has been much more influential than its size would indicate by leveraging its intellectual resources in strategy, organization, governance, relevant content and case study preparation, devising award schemes and training a broad range of people as award judges for consistent and objective application of the award criteria, and marketing the success stories to promote the supporters of the cause to mobilize further resources, thereby establishing a virtuous cycle.

While most of the contributions are indirect, ARGE Consulting has been the catalyst, methodology developer, recruiter, and motivator of many significant initiatives that have served the community in a meaningful way.

ARGE consultants have also taken leadership positions such as Chairman and/or board members of several NGOs, and particularly on the nominating committees of each to ensure sustainability of leadership and governance for these initiatives. The fact that all these NGOs are among the most credible NGOs due to their effectiveness and transparency (as all have their accounts audited by independent third parties and publish their results), is a result of the emphasis put on their governance systems by ARGE.

ARGE has earned recognition in Europe as a leader in "shaping the future" with the effectiveness of its pro bono public work and as a benchmark for the business world showing commitment to its community through social responsibility projects. ARGE's work is also being used as a case study in various universities in Turkiye and abroad.

A SECTORAL DEPLOYMENT STRATEGY FOR THE UN GLOBAL COMPACT

What changes the world is not armies, arms, or economic power, but the power of ideas. The greatest revolutions, whether they be social, scientific, or economic in nature, have occurred because of the introduction of a new idea and its dissemination. The faster an idea is disseminated and adopted, the faster and more consequential the change will be. In today's world due to technologies that facilitate the sharing and communication of ideas, technical obstacles to the dissemination of ideas are dwindling. On the other hand, the sheer volume of new ideas reaching people makes it harder to arouse curiosity or to remember all. Therefore, it is as important to market ideas as it is to produce them in order to instigate change.

UN's Global Compact (GC) is an example of such an idea. In 1999, at Davos, Mr. Kofi Annan, the Secretary General of the UN at the time, called the leaders individually and collectively to "embrace, support and enact a set of core values in the areas of human rights, labor standards, environmental practices," and to combat corruption. In July of 2000, the UN formally initiated the Global Compact to call for voluntary participation of all kinds of institutions to advance their commitments to sustainability and corporate citizenship. What was novel about this call was its **voluntary nature**, albeit with a **condition to submit a public report** on each institution's annual implementation of the ten universally accepted principles.

The Global Compact has become a leadership platform, endorsed by Chief Executive Officers, and offering a unique strategic platform for participants to advance their commitments to sustainability and corporate citizenship. The requirement to communicate openly and honestly about the activities, successes, and challenges of the participating institutions has been a critical impetus for not only continuous improvement of their own performances, but also as a means to set benchmarks and to share best-in-class examples globally. Performance, if not measured, cannot be seen to have improved. Global Compact, despite its voluntary nature, has not only increased the focus on measuring performance in key sustainability areas, but has also increased their priority in the eyes of institutional leaders as they had to publicly report progress on an annual basis.

While some criticize the lack of third party verification of the annual Communications on Progress (COP) each institution prepares, many companies are starting to incorporate such independent reviews, once again voluntarily, in order to increase the credibility of their reporting. In short, **public reporting brings its own discipline and motivation for continuous improvement**.

One of the key dilemmas for businesses is whether they are responsible to their shareholders or to all of their stakeholders, including the workers, customers, other members of the value chain, and even the community in which they operate. In reality, this is a false dilemma. This is so because responsible behavior of a company in a society is key to its sustainability. Responsible corporate citizenship actually benefits the shareholders. Trust is the foundation of sustainable development. As the world continues to get smaller, our mutual interdependence increases and we all need to be able to mobilize others' resources and goodwill to achieve success. Mobilizing others' resources can only be achieved through gaining their trust. Therefore, the ability to gain the trust of global financial markets and all the stakeholders in the value chain is becoming the key to success. The Global Compact, through voluntary declaration of the performance about the relationships with all stakeholders, provides an opportunity to improve the trust for the corporation, if these declarations are sincere. However, by the same process of annual public declarations, it increases the risk of not being transparent and sincere, by making it easier to identify inconsistencies of behavior.

Therefore, common goals, such as building markets, combating corruption, safeguarding the environment, and ensuring social inclusion, have resulted in unprecedented partnerships and openness among business, government, civil society, labor, and the UN. Global Compact has become the largest corporate citizenship and sustainability initiative in the world with over 8,000 participants from more than 130 countries. In short, Global Compact provides a tool for self-enforcing discipline to be a responsible corporate citizen, thereby improving social license to operate and be sustainable to participating institutions.

During its first decade, the efforts to increase the number of participants in Global Compact have been organized on a national basis and without a focus on specific industries. The same applies to the GC Local Network (GCLN) in Turkiye as well. The Turkish Network is governed by a multistakeholder body represented by some of the largest Turkish companies, SMEs, and NGOs.[2] One of the key goals established by this body was to increase the effectiveness of deployment of the UN Global Compact (UNGC). Under the leadership of ARGE Consulting (the first Turkish signatory of the UNGC) Turkish GC Local Network has initiated a new sector specific approach to deployment of the UNGC that was recommended to other countries' local networks at the Leadership Summit in June 2010 in New York.

Segmentation is a key marketing concept. A market segment is a sub-set of a market made up of organizations sharing one or more characteristics that cause them to demand similar product and/or services based on qualities of those products such as price or function. A good market segmentation ensures that the chosen sub-set of the market has different needs than other segments (*distinct*), is homogeneous within the segment (*common needs*), can be reached by a similar approach, and *responds similarly* to a stimulus.

GCLN Turkiye has embarked on a new **Sector Specific Approach** to utilize the market segmentation idea for deployment of the GC. Companies in a specific sector tend to face common issues distinct from other sectors. Also, it is easier to reach companies of a particular sector through their industry associations. Finally, collective action enables a comradeship approach within the industry and convincing leading players of the sector increases the attractiveness to join the GC to avoid being left behind.

Three main sectors were selected: pharmaceutical, automotive, and textiles due to their importance in the Turkish economy. Initially focusing on these three key sectors, the GCLN Turkiye organized various outreach events to increase the number of signatories, brainstorming sessions with the aim of increasing a consciousness of the universal principles of the Global Compact and identifying key sector issues with their application, and training sessions to improve COP quality, share best-in-class examples, and ultimately to ensure effective implementation of Global Compact principles by the companies in the sector.

The purpose of this Sector Specific Approach is to:

- make sure that the awareness for ten GC principles is increased throughout the sector;
- identify issues specific to the sector in implementing the ten GC principles and to ask sector representatives to propose solutions for implementation;
- ensure that leading companies within the sector to sign the GC and be a role model for the sector;
- initiate a sector wide impetus to increase number of signatories collectively;
- promote best-in-class benchmarks as role models to increase implementation of GC principles;
- incorporate sector associations and labor organizations to support implementation of GC principles;
- identify sector specific standards, rules, and regulations that may help in implementing the GC principles.

This Sector Specific Approach is being implemented in three key industries: pharmaceutical, automotive, and textile. The reasons for this selection are:

- that each sector employs of a large number of people;
- they are critically important in the competitiveness of the Turkish economy;
- they have a broad geographic presence;
- international standards in these industries are significant;
- because of their export potential.

The implementation of this Sector Specific Approach involves:

1. identification of a key player in the industry who could become a role model for the rest of the companies in this industry;
2. identification of sector associations, foundations, and other key stakeholders;
3. invitation of these key players for a workshop where GC principles and good practices in implementation are shared;
4. asking the sector representatives to identify sector specific issues based on each of the ten GC principles and to provide potential solutions;
5. preparing a summary report based on this workshop and sharing it widely within the sector;
6. inviting interested parties to a public signing ceremony for GC principles and publicizing the event to introduce a sense of urgency and competitive tension between companies;
7. whenever necessary, providing support for preparation of COPs and sharing benchmark examples within the industry to promote right behaviors.

The purpose of the workshops was to involve all interested parties and sector representatives in identifying key issues for this specific sector in applying GC principles in this industry. The participants were first given a presentation by experts on all four key areas of the GC: human rights, labor, environment, and anticorruption. The presentations also included some benchmark examples either from other industries or from other countries.

The next step was to conduct a "brainstorming" exercise in small groups to identify the issues and challenges of applying each of the GC principles in the specific sector. The second step was to prioritize these issues and try to identify potential solution to these challenges. The third step was to identify other institutions that may help overcome these difficulties, projects that maybe undertaken jointly with industry participants to help resolve these issues, as well as approximate timing and resource requirements to overcome the identified sector-specific challenges.

Such a report identifying sector-specific issues and potential solutions along with a schedule of implementation and resource requirements is a key content development effort that helps all stakeholders to understand more fully, assess, and implement GC principles. It also has the effect of mobilizing collective efforts within the industry by promoting a common understanding.

A collective effort by the GCLN and industry associations and having a formal signing ceremony with government representatives and the media promotes a sense of urgency and an impetus to enlist. Also, utilizing key industry players' willingness to be part of the GC to create a platform to share their views about the GC attracts the attention of the media and other industry participants. Finally such a public show brings energy to the movement and a discipline for implementation throughout the year. Such a public commitment is the key to effective implementation of GC principles.

By involving industry organizations, key players, and industry leaders GCLN Turkiye created a momentum to join and implement GC principles in specific industries. Companies tend to follow the developments within their own industry more closely than they followed general trends. Therefore, enlisting leading players within an industry to GC principles has a positive pulling-in effect on most of the industry participants. In particular, involving industry organizations in this effort makes it easier to raise awareness throughout the sector. Also, being specific about the challenges of implementation for a particular industry enhances collective action to resolve some common issues and promotes broad participation and effective implementation. Finally, industry specific benchmarks and good practice examples are more meaningful for industry participants and enables multicountry comparisons.

As a result of this approach, for example, in the pharmaceutical industry while there were only 84 signatories of the UNGC within the first decade throughout the world, 33 pharmaceutical companies signed the UNGC in Turkiye at the start.

In short, applying the concept of market segmentation to implement a Sector Specific Approach to the deployment of GC principles is an effective way to broaden the reach of GC and improve the effectiveness of implementation of GC principles.

BENEFITS OF VOLUNTARY WORK

Individuals who believe in providing input to shape their own future, human rights, and democracy should actively support NGOs. Through NGOs, citizens should interact with the international community. Governments should not regard NGOs as competitors or impediments, but rather as resources whose input should be encouraged and supported.

Voluntary work satisfies an individual's need to be valuable, and making a contribution to his community without any compensation expectation is one way of meeting this need. In the private sector experience, those who are involved in voluntary work report positive developments in their motivation, the gaining of new skills, becoming part of a new circle of people, and an increase in their self-confidence and self-satisfaction from making a difference and being of service.

If all segments of society in a country subscribe to the notion of participatory democracy and make the concept a part of their lives, the country will play a leading role in addressing global issues.

NGO CONTRIBUTION TO THE BUSINESS WORLD

NGOs are not only at the receiving end in such a relationship. The fact that NGO management is not simple may also provide learning opportunities for the private sector. NGO management is not simple for the following reasons:

1. goals related to social issues are complicated to resolve;
2. human or financial resources are limited, no remunerative sanctions are possible, and a lot of energy is required to maintain high motivation levels;
3. raising finances requires enormous creativity;
4. resolutions to social issues require intensive interaction with different segments of society, therefore managing a network of relationships is an important part of NGO success.

NGOs understand the need to devise their mission and vision in a participatory manner. Generating resources, focusing them to achieve results, maintaining focus against differing demands requires the mission and the vision to be set in a participatory manner. This is the key to maintain the volunteer spirit and mobilize resources, and where NGOs can set an example to the business world.

Successful NGOs know that goodwill cannot replace good management. Therefore they take care to match volunteer skills with goals when making assignments. In the case of KalDer, management effectiveness is maintained by the custom that board members are high-level managers of leading companies in quality management. Similarly, training the volunteers to improve their skills increases their effectiveness and motivation.

Here again there are lessons to be learned from NGOs in managing the modern day employees. Volunteer management requires that they are trained, given assignments that will stretch and excite them, and that their achievements are recognized.

In short, NGOs are critical instruments of improving governance by improving channels of participation.

NOTES

1   Turkish name for the Corporate Volunteers Association is Ozel Sektor Gonulluler Dernegi (OSGD) see www.osgd.org.
2   The Turkish Global Compact Network is governed by a steering committee representing multistakeholders. The members of the Steering Committee are representatives of ARGE Consulting, Aksa Akrilik, Koc Holding, Sabanci Holding, TISK, TUSIAD, and Zed Tanitim (three of the largest Turkish companies, two SMEs, and two NGOs).

CHAPTER 6

Governance for Sustainability of Corporations: Continuous Creation of Value

Improving quality of management improves quality of life.

'Imagination is more important than knowledge.' (Albert Einstein).

Corporations command a significant part of global resources, create value for customers throughout the world, and have an influence over an even larger number of people through their influence on their stakeholders. Therefore, their ability to create value for their stakeholders and their sustainability is important for improving quality of life.

The essence of good corporate governance is ensuring trustworthy relations between the corporation and its stakeholders. Corporations that flourish through the use of the world's resources are becoming increasingly aware that they need to be accountable toward all parties that have a stake in those resources. As our dependence on global resources increases, we need to be aware of the need to have our governance systems and attitudes gain a global dimension. Today, successful and sustainable organizations need to demonstrate a willingness to involve stakeholders in decision making, to embrace a culture of transparency and accountability, to be fair and consistent in relations with stakeholders, and to have an organizational infrastructure that ensures "corporate trust."

Trust is the foundation of success. It is at the foundation of all relationships. As the world continues to get smaller, the interdependence between corporations and their stakeholders grows larger. Companies who earn the trust of their stakeholders are able to mobilize more resources throughout their value chain to achieve sustainable success. This is the fundamental reason why good corporate governance is being embraced by companies in diverse industries, small and large, publicly or privately owned, throughout the world.

Good corporate governance is the key to attracting financial and human capital to the corporation, strong business partners to the value chain, and ensuring sustainability of value creation.

To compete globally, companies are becoming more and more dependent on international credit or equity capital markets. Similarly, as their influence on the development of world economy increases, companies' area of responsibility also grows beyond their own shareholders to include society as a whole as stakeholders. As the management quality of a company is determined as much by the quality of its corporate structure as it is by the quality of its managers, the trustworthiness of this structure is critical to financial markets as well as to all other stakeholders that it deals with.

Even though there is no single recipe for ensuring good corporate governance, there are some widely accepted practices. Appointment of two different people for Chairman and CEO to ensure checks and balances in a manner similar to developed democracies, and hiring independent third parties for financial audit are examples of such practices.

Timely, simultaneous, and adequate disclosure of easy to understand and standard information to all stakeholders is increasingly becoming the norm for gaining trust. Fairness to all stakeholders, and not differentiating among small and large shareholders, regardless of whether they are represented on the board, is a key parameter.

Events leading to the recent economic crisis and recession show that numerous companies were either not aware of the risks they were carrying, or were risking the company. Also, compensation arrangements for key executives were not aligned with the long-term performance of these companies. Clearly these institutions faced serious governance failures, with many boards falling short in their two key areas of responsibility: guidance and oversight.

To remedy this situation, many governments are considering new regulations – just as the Sarbanes-Oxley regulations came in the wake of the Enron incident. Even though good intentions may be behind this new regulatory impetus, we should not forget that regulation alone cannot bring good governance. In fact, **excessive regulation brings the threat of overwhelming bureaucracy, which stifles innovation and risk taking. A better remedy would be to increase the diversity of the boards.**

Even the widely admired, number one car manufacturer Toyota, which introduced management concepts like "lean manufacturing" to the world, is not immune from governance lapses.

Toyota has a 29 member Board of Directors. Yet, the Toyota's Board has no women and no non-Japanese Directors. All members are Toyota insiders, and there are no independent members. Similarly, out of their top 50 executives, Toyota has no women and only 10% are non-Japanese members. This management insularity and homogeneity is one of the reasons for the Toyota's blind spot and failure to address on a timely basis the problem that led to the recall of some 8 million cars for unintended acceleration.

History is full of examples where insular, homogeneous groups reinforce prevailing attitudes and conventional wisdom, resulting in groupthink and failure to adapt to new challenges. Furthermore, Toyota's culture of secrecy led to complacency and a lack of transparency, which are significant governance failures. As the *Economist* put it "If Toyota's board had included, say, a female German boss, a former American senator and a high-flying Hong Kong lawyer, its response to the crisis might have been different."[1] In short, the response to the problem (or more appropriately the lack thereof), turned out to be a bigger problem. Hence, bringing complementary skills and experience to the boards is valuable for the sustainability of the corporations.

DIVERSITY AT THE HEAD TABLE

A key function of boards of directors is to ensure that the risks taken by management on behalf of the shareholders are consistent and balanced, and that they have a high likelihood of value creation. To be sustainable, an organization must strike a fine balance between:

- risk and reward;
- short and long term;
- interests of various stakeholders;
- ethical considerations and market practices;
- providing effective oversight versus motivating management to assume calculated risks for value creation.

To achieve this balance, an organization needs an effective process for challenging management decisions, particularly those involving strategic choices that inherently involve risk taking. It is very difficult to accomplish this objective by regulation. The need is for a well-functioning board of directors.

However, as the world has changed, so has the definition of a *well-functioning board*. Just as no single individual – regardless of capabilities – is likely to be sufficient in striking the right balance in all the areas listed above, neither can a *group* of individuals who differ little from each other. Gone are the days when a cadre of like-minded older men with similar résumés could provide adequate guidance and oversight for a company. The critical need today is for diversity of experience and perspectives. If everybody thinks the same on all matters, then there is no need for a board; one individual would suffice! A good team needs players with complementary skills and the ability to work together.

IMPORTANT AREAS OF DIVERSITY

Generally, we tend to think of diversity in the context of *gender* or *ethnicity*. However, to build a strong team, boards should also consider *diversity of skills and experience, age distribution, and tenure*. Diversity for its own sake is not an improvement in governance; what matters is the combination of *complementary* skills and experiences that members bring to the table to address better the challenges the company is likely to face.

Diversity of Skills and Experience

The diversity of skills and experience can be broken down into: *industry experience*; *geographic experience, religions and nationalities*; *functional experience*; *stakeholder experience*; and *experience with different business scales* and *stages of business life cycles*.

Industry experience

In light of the increase in cross links between different industries, having broad industry experience on a board is becoming more relevant than deeper expertise in a single industry. For example, the board members of Nestlé do not come solely from the food industry. Their experience in different industries enables them to address issues that are important to Nestlé, such as following new trends closely (politics, academia), understanding the needs of youth (technology, multimedia), understanding capital and credit markets (banking, finance), and focusing on health and beauty (pharmaceutical, cosmetics). Although the board members come from different fields (see Table 6.1), they all have senior management experience and possess the skills to guide and to provide oversight to the company.[2]

Geographic experience, religions and nationalities

With so many companies expanding throughout the world, it is increasingly important for different nationalities to be represented on boards of directors. These boards need to understand the global nature of the risks and potential rewards of doing business. In many

Table 6.1 Nestlé Board of Directors (2007)

Name	Position	Industry
Peter Brabeck-Latmanthe	Chairman and CEO, Nestlé	
Adreas Koopmann	CEO, Bobst Group	Packaging (carton, etc.)
Rolf Hanggi	Deputy Chairman, Roche	Pharmaceutical
Edward George	Former Member, Bank of England	Finance
Kaspar Villiger	Former Minister, Switzerland	Politics
Jean-Pierre Meyers	Deputy Chairman, L'Oreal	Cosmetics
Peter Böckli	Attorney	Legal
Andre Kudelski	Chairman and CEO, Kudelski Group	Technology (digital safety)
Daniel Borel	Chairman, Logitech	Technology (computers, etc.)
Carolina Müller-Möhl	Chairman, Müller-Möhl Group	Asset Management
Günter Bobel	Professor, Rockefeller University	Academician
Jean-Rene Fourtou	Chairman, Vivendi Universal	Multimedia (TV, music, etc.)
Steven George Hoch	Partner, Highmount Capital	Investment Management
Niana Lal Kidwai	CEO, HSBC India	Finance (banking)

Source: ARGE Consulting research based on Nestlé Annual Report, 2007.

instances beliefs of people have a significant impact on their behaviors and purchasing decisions. In particular, their dependency on emerging markets, such as BRIC[3] or Next Eleven,[4] is growing in importance. Yet, most boards do not have a sufficiently diverse membership to keep pace with this trend. Table 6.2 shows that even some of the most significant global companies, whose assets span a broad geographic domain, lack diversity in the nationalities of their board members.

By broadening the board-member recruitment base to include emerging countries, an organization increases its ability to recruit highly qualified individuals who are generally missed in traditional board membership search processes. Boards of *global* companies in particular need to recruit members from more diverse national backgrounds. A firm that is making a significant investment in a new geography or targeting significant growth in a new emerging market, for instance, can benefit from having board members with relevant[5] experience in that geographic region.

The Turkish market provides an example. Many Turkish companies are increasing their international presence, especially in Russia, Central Asia, Middle East, and Eastern Europe. According to the Turkish Corporate Governance Association's website (http://www.tkyd.org) many companies are voluntarily attaining independent ratings for the ISE (Istanbul Stock Exchange) Corporate Governance Index. Of the companies with the top rankings (8.25–10.00) – Anadolu Efes,[6] Coca

Table 6.2 Insufficient Geographic Diversity on Company Boards

Company Name	Foreign Assets 2008, ($ bn)	% of total assets in foreign countries	No. of Board Mem. Male	Female	Nationality of Board Members
GE[a]	400	50	13	3	13 American, 2 Canadian, 1 British
Royal Dutch Shell[b]	230	79	12	1	5 British, 3 Dutch, 2 Swiss, 1 Finnish, 1 French, 1 American
Vodafone[c]	200	92	11	1	5 British, 2 French, 1 Italian, 1 New Zealander, 1 Belgian, 1 South African,
BP[d]	188	83	12	2	9 British, 4 American, 1 Swedish,
Toyota[e]	168	57	29	0	All Japanese
Exxon Mobile[f]	162	71	8	2	All American
Total[g]	146	86	13	2	12 French, 1 Swedish, 1 Canadian, 1 British
E.ON[h]	139	65	5	1	5 German, 1 Norwegian
EDF[i]	135	48	16	2	16 French, 1 British, 1 Moroccan
ArcelorMittal[j]	130	96	16	1	4 Luxembourg, 4 French, 3 Indian, 2 American, 2 Spanish, 1 Belgian, 1 Brazilian
Volkswagen[k]	127	53	7	0	5 German, 1 Austrian, 1 Spanish
GDF Suez[l]	122	51	18	3	18 French, 1 Belgian, 1 Canadian, 1 British

Notes: a. GE's 2009 Annual Report; b. Royal Dutch Shell 2009 Annual Report; c. Vodafone 2009 Annual Report; d. BP 2009 Annual Reports and Accounting 2009; e. Toyota Annual Report 2009; f. Exxon 2009 Annual Report; g. Total Factbook 2009; h. E.On http://www.eon.com/en/investors/14272.jsp; i. EDF Annual Performance Report 2009; j. ArcelorMittal. http:// boldfuturelive.thoburns.com/boardofdirectors.php; k. Volkswagen 2009 Annual Report; l. GDF Suez http://google.brand.edgar-online.com/EFX_dll/EDGARpro.dll?FetchFilingHTML1?ID=6666424&SessionID=uYwUH6nEJqqdjz7 , http://www.gdfsuez.com/en/group/governance/board-of-directors/biographies/biographies/.

Sources: The first three columns are from *The Economist* (July 29, 2010), next three columns from on ARGE Consulting research.

Cola Icecek, Dogan Yayin Holding, Hurriyet, TAV, Tupras, and Vestel – all except Tupras[7] and Vestel have international board members. Many of these companies also have significant international operations. It is interesting to note that many of the major Turkish companies that did not get a corporate governance rating – such as Sabanci Holding, Dogus Holding, Ulker,[8] and Eczacibasi Holding – do not have any international board members. From this, **there appears to be a correlation between Turkish companies' international ambitions and the presence of international diversity on their boards.**

Functional experience

There have always been certain attributes that all board members need to possess, and that has not changed.[9] However, as today's corporations face issues that are more and more complex, it is increasingly important that they have board members with specialized knowledge. Expertise in specific areas – such as the legal framework, capital markets, technological developments, and social trends relevant to the corporation – improves the quality and effectiveness of the board.

A company developing new Internet technologies, for instance, would significantly benefit from having board members who understand intellectual property protection and who have served on the boards of other high-tech start-ups. For example, a Turkish company, Borusan Telecom (an alternate phone operator), improved the experience of its board by recruiting a former senior executive from British Telecom, a private equity investor, and a business strategist.[10] This choice of board members proved to be useful in developing a sound company, and in eventually marketing the company to Vodafone.

Stakeholder experience

Stakeholders such as governmental bodies, environmental groups, trade associations, unions, communities, and the public at large are becoming more influential in matters related to the business world. Therefore, an understanding of the concerns and inner workings of these key stakeholders is useful in guiding the corporation during the process of developing and implementing appropriate strategies. In regulated industries, for example, it is helpful to have a board member who understands the regulatory agency, its mentality, and its processes.

The increased importance being placed on the interests of all stakeholders, as opposed to a single-minded focus on shareholders, is also apparent in the Turkish governance world. Stakeholder issues are becoming a regular part of board debate. For example, Turkiye hosts one of the largest local networks of the UN Global Compact.[11] Furthermore, 12 of the top 20 groups and two of the largest Chambers of Commerce and Industry have become members of the Global Compact.

Competitive strategy requires an understanding of not only the players of the industry in which a company competes, but also its suppliers,

customers, potential substitutes, and new entrants, as well as the shifting trends in technology and in the regulatory environment. Therefore, having people with diverse stakeholder experiences helps improve board decision making. Yet, it is critical that board members are not viewed – either by themselves or by their peers – as representing a particular stakeholder, but rather as key members of the team that make up the board. This understanding is critical in ensuring that their ties to the stakeholders do not create conflicts of interest with the company.

Since every individual is involved in numerous relationships, having one – especially a successful one – with a current or potential stakeholder of the company cannot and should not be a justification for removing a candidate from the eligibility list due to a theoretical potential conflict. What is important is how the candidate behaves if and when there is a potential area of conflict, and the best guide is the track record of the individual. Evaluating the independence of individual members is a delicate task that needs to be performed on a regular basis, particularly by the peers, based on the behavior and judgment of the individual under different circumstances.

Experience with different business scales and stages of business life cycles

Businesses continually develop new products and new markets. At their inception stage, these businesses are generally a small size. Yet, in many cases they represent the future of the corporation and so should receive sufficient attention. It is helpful to have board members who understand the needs of small or start-up businesses.

Board members who have experience with relevant stages of the business life cycle can be a real asset, particularly during a transition. A good board at the entrepreneurial stage may not have the necessary skills for a company at maturity. If a company is planning to list its shares on a public exchange, for example, before starting such a process it would be prudent to appoint a few board members who have experience on the boards of publicly listed companies. Similarly, if a company is going to make a significant investment that is much larger than its previous investments, recruiting board members with megaproject experience would be very beneficial.

Diversity of Age Distribution

To be sustainable, corporations need board members of different ages. With today's rapid changes in technology and social trends comes the need to have younger board members who are able to identify potential risks and remedies associated with these changes. For example, understanding technical trading, hedge funds, or option agreements that pose significant risks requires a grasp of mathematical modeling that few older-generation executives have. Also, **understanding of the potential of Internet marketing is much deeper in the new generation. Hence, companies that recruit younger board members with sufficiently broad and holistic experience are benefiting from their decisions.**

Age diversity also allows for an easier transition when people retire from the board, since having a range of ages makes it less likely that a large proportion of the members will be retiring at once. A mix of ages helps ensure that there will be a sufficient number of experienced board members.

However, for diversity of age distribution to be genuinely beneficial, new or younger members must demonstrate intellectual independence and, when necessary, stand up to the older ones. This level of participation is critical for a balanced board. If all the members cannot be considered as peers, because one or more members enjoy a distinct advantage over others due to sector knowledge or management experience, some members may refrain from expressing their opinions. Such a situation seriously damages the intellectual independence of the whole board.

Diversity of Tenure on the Board

Another area that requires careful balance is diversity of tenure. One of the key responsibilities of boards is to prevent potential conflicts of interest between the management and the shareholders. Clear separation of management rights (taking initiative and implementation) and governance rights (guidance, approval, and oversight) is critical in minimizing potential "agency" risks of the management, such as:

- fraud;
- cronyism (building a personal fiefdom with company resources);
- lethargy (focusing on excuses as opposed to results);
- being too risk-averse (potentially leading to overinvestment);
- being too risk-prone (betting the company).

A thorough knowledge of the business, as well as of the strengths and weaknesses of the management team helps address these risks and maintain a healthy balance.

On the other hand, as people become familiar with each other, their tendency to challenge each other diminishes. Therefore, having diversity of tenure on the board, with both relatively new and old members, keeps the board members sharp and helps them address these issues properly.

Ethnic and Gender Diversity[12]

Broadening the ethnic and gender diversity of boards not only helps increase the size of the candidate pool and therefore the quality of potential board members, but it also helps broaden the perspectives and experience of the whole team. Having more than a token female or minority member – and making sure that such members are deemed peers, by recruiting really qualified people – improves the tone of boards significantly.

Board dynamics work through conversation, body language, and argument, and all participants need to learn the spoken and unspoken rules of the game. It is not sufficient just to recruit women and minorities; there also must be a positive environment of candor and openness if minorities and women are to operate as effective board members.

Women represent a significant part of the work force and of the customer base of most companies. Yet, with a few notable exceptions such as Norway, their representation on boards is lacking. Studies reveal a number of potential benefits of having more women on boards, such as better financial performance, increased focus on risk management, better understanding of consumer markets, stronger organizational performance, and better investor confidence. A closer discussion of each of these benefits follows.

Superior financial performance

Research indicates that companies with women on their boards are more profitable than their peers. Companies with at least three women on their boards experience greater *total return to shareholders, return on invested capital*, and *return on equity*. In 2009, Fortune 500 companies in the top 25% of female representation reported:[13]

- 66% higher return on invested capital;
- 42% greater return on sales;
- 53% higher return on equity.

Increased focus on risk management

Likewise, companies with women board members deal more effectively with risk. For example boards with more women focus on:

- risk management by addressing the issues and concerns of their customers, employees, shareholders, and local community; and

- the direction and long-term priorities of a company, hence mitigating and controlling risk.

Greater understanding of the consumer market

Companies with women on boards are better equipped to develop products and services that appeal to all of their customers. Reasons are identified below:

- women currently drive 70% of purchasing decisions in the European Union and 80% in the United States;
- women now represent a growing proportion of the consumer base, even in industries where buyers traditionally are male;[14]
- women are in tune with the needs of other women, which can help foster innovation and differentiate companies from their competitors;
- women address global trends that organizations have ranked as most important in the future:

  1) a faster pace of technological innovation;
  2) an increasing availability of knowledge;
  3) a greater competition for talent.[15]

Stronger organizational performance

Research indicates a positive link between women on boards and stronger organizational performance. Examples follow:

- a woman on a board signals that a company takes seriously the views of its diverse stakeholders;
- female directors serve as role models for other women in their companies, and thereby improve the performance of female employees, boost the company's brand image, and strengthen customer and employee satisfaction;
- women practice collaborative and open leadership styles at board meetings, which leads to informed decisions and innovation.[16]

Greater investor confidence

Evidence suggests that investor confidence improves with the addition of women to a company's board. For instance:

- more investment fund companies, such as CalPERS and PAX World Funds, are including gender diversity indicators among their criteria;

- it is likely that the rising number of female investors will want to invest with companies that promote gender representation as a part of board diversity;
- rating agencies are adding gender diversity criteria to evaluate a company's strategies and corporate governance, because they view gender representation as a source of organizational excellence and performance.[17]

MANAGING DIVERSITY

While diversity improves governance, building a well-functioning team from individuals with diverse skills and experience requires that the board be properly managed – a key role for the chairman, who needs to pay attention to the following points:

- **Trust** – a high level of mutual respect, trust, and candor must exist among all board members. A culture of transparency and openness – and the discipline to prepare sufficiently for meetings – is essential to creating an environment of trust. Members should be able to trust each other with the unity of their values and goals, as well as with their ability to contribute to the business of the corporation.
- **Communication** – even if each team member is a competent and senior individual, establishing an environment of trust requires spending time together and exchanging ideas and views. The most important tool for developing communication and team spirit is ensuring access to relevant and meaningful information in a timely and synchronous fashion. If the management treats different board members differently regarding the provision of information, it will damage the climate of trust.
- **Teamwork** – the board has to work as a unified team, not as individual stars. The differentiation of members based on their background, and especially the creation of a feeling of "insiders" (say, family members) and "the rest" is harmful to team spirit. The board should focus on value creation for the company and act as a team, not just as individuals.
- **Incentives** – corporate incentive systems should be set up so as to increase team performance. From this perspective, board remuneration should also be team-based.
- **Vision** – the board should invest sufficient time to ensure agreement on a common vision. Also, a comprehensive orientation program for board members is an effective way to make sure

they understand the environment and the competencies of the company.

- **Rotating responsibilities** – planned changes are necessary to ensure lasting team success. From time to time, responsibilities within the board need to be changed; team performance can be enhanced through the introduction of new team members.

STEPS TOWARD DIVERSITY

Diversity in the boardroom strengthens the capacity to strike the right balance on numerous dimensions that the board must consider for the sustainability of the organization. To improve diversity on the board, we need to take certain steps:

1. **Identify challenges** – identify the top few challenges that the firm is expected to face over the next few years, and question whether the board collectively has sufficient experience to adequately assess the risks associated with these challenges.

2. **Identify a broad pool of candidates** – focus on preparing the best pool of potential candidates to fill the gaps identified during the first step. Traditionally, members of boards of directors are picked by the largest shareholder, the chairman, or the CEO. The personal connections of the largest shareholder or CEO may in fact be useful in attracting valuable members to the board, but it also increases the risk of a board composed of "acquaintances" who may hesitate to challenge the CEO. Also, not having a specific process to establish a wide enough pool of potential candidates may discourage accomplished individuals from joining the board, and thus limit the diversity of experience.

   Boards must actively seek out skilled and competent candidates and ensure that sufficient diversity of experience is brought to the board. Since it is difficult for the full board to conduct such a search, this process is generally the responsibility of the corporate governance committee. However, the final decision should be made by the full board, with the benefit of the committee's work. It may also be helpful to rely on the expertise of specialists in this area when seeking out new independent board members. The search process should provide an open-minded approach to reach a wide pool of candidates. **Evaluation of candidates should be based on their competencies as board members, as well as their fit to the team, their potential to help with the issues facing the company, and their contribution to the diversity of the**

board. One other consideration is the ability of the candidates to provide sufficient time and attention to the board. For example, a member who is a CEO of another corporation should not be expected to take on more than two or three independent board membership positions.

3. **Establish a diversity culture** – make good use of the diversity. To prevent complacency and groupthink on the board, maintain a climate of candor and openness, and encourage members to voice different opinions. Use team-building exercises to make sure the board members spend time together and have an opportunity to appreciate each others' perspectives and wisdom. To provide appropriate guidance and oversight, focus not only on business results but also on sustainability issues and risk management techniques, such as scenario planning.

4. **Conduct regular reviews to learn and improve** – conduct self-appraisals on a regular basis, and take appropriate measures when deficiencies are identified, either to modify behavior or to change the composition of the board.

Challenges that companies face are becoming more complex – geographically, technologically, and socially. If boards are going to be able to provide the right kind of guidance and oversight in this rapidly diversifying climate, increased diversity at the head table is imperative.

Unity in goals and values, plus diversity in perspectives and experience, enriches the quality of decision making.

ROLE OF THE BOARD OF DIRECTORS

The most important element of organizational structure is the board of directors. The board has the ultimate decision making power and therefore the ultimate responsibility toward the stakeholders and for the sustainability of the corporation.

The board does not run the company. Rather they provide guidance and advice to the management, veto decisions they deem inappropriate, and make changes to the management team if and when they see fit. The board's responsibility is providing guidance and oversight to the management in order to ensure that the company creates value on a sustainable basis while protecting the interests of all stakeholders.

The best and basic way for companies to benefit from good corporate management is to appoint capable and independent board members. Consequently, the competencies and experience of the board members, their ability to remain independent and to adhere to principles of good governance bear great importance to the institutions' success and sustainability. Issues such as the composition, the agenda, the processes of the board, and how the board develops its own effectiveness as a team ensure the quality of governance of the company.

Having a board with sufficiently diverse experience, and critical and independent thinking skills to challenge the various strategic choices increases the probability of success in a company.

EXPECTATIONS OF BOARD MEMBERS

A board must be provided with appropriate members, structure, and processes to ensure that it can fulfill its main duties of guidance, decision making, and oversight. In fulfilling its fiduciary duties, board members need to be not only competent but also sufficiently informed to make judgments about the sustainability of the company. Furthermore, this is not done by taking over the role of the management but rather by ensuring the management of the company takes the necessary actions and decisions with this understanding.

First and foremost, board members must have a good knowledge of the corporation and its market. Knowledge of the corporation's past and current positioning, strengths and weaknesses, threats and opportunities, culture and potential, is critically important for providing guidance and oversight.

The board members should have a good grasp of the corporation's circumstances and use this knowledge to implement a challenging and constructive questioning process to ensure that every aspect of a decision is considered.

They must also have a good understanding of the cash flow of the corporation. Cash flow is more vital to a company than profitability. Inconsistencies that may arise between the cash situation and profitability must be particularly well understood. If for instance an increase in sales volume is achieved by extension of longer credit terms, it increases the working capital requirement, reduces profitability and increases the risk profile of the company, and therefore the credit policy must be reevaluated.

It is important to compare corporation performance not only against prior years or budget numbers, but also with the performance of competitors. Such comparisons must not be limited to their financial results, but also other productivity indicators such as, customer, supplier, and employer satisfaction and strategic initiatives. As far as productivity indicators, a comparison of processes to benchmark examples serves as a good vehicle for improvement.

Board members should concern themselves not only with the current performance of the corporation, but also with its future. They should pay particular attention to those risk areas that may impact corporation performance, and ensure that these risks are determined and managed. Organizing meetings to conduct various scenario analyses facilitates mental preparation of members and management for dealing with these risk factors should they arise.

Another important area of concern is succession planning. Unexpected changes in key management are a risk factor for the corporation. Therefore board members must pay attention not only to the performance of management, but also to succession planning. This process involves both identifying and following internal and external candidates as well as establishing development plans for internal candidates.

Another important concern for the future of the corporation is how it will grow, and what risks it will have to assume to achieve this growth. Board members have to be up to date in their information and understanding of the takeover targets and risks associated with the market.

Off balance sheet liabilities is another area that requires special attention by the board of directors. Whether on written or oral basis, any undertakings by the corporation must be carefully monitored. Therefore the board must regularly review the agreements with distributors, remuneration arrangements with top management, and any other third party agreements.

Companies are evaluated not only according to their financial results but also according to legal requirements and ethical expectations. The establishment of a continuous monitoring system and systematic review by an internal audit department that has direct access to the board are important. Also, having a dependable whistle blowing process is useful in identifying potential risks of fraud. Board members should have sufficient contact with management and employees at different levels to evaluate the risks.

Occasional interaction of board members with customers increases their grasp of corporation's service and product quality versus customer expectations, and hence contributes to their judgment and input.

A sound understanding of each link in the value chain and its alternatives, and where the value added is captured throughout the entire system (suppliers, sales channels, and so on) is useful in making appropriate assessments of the corporation's risks. The strength of a chain is determined by the strength of its weakest link.

Companies do not operate in a vacuum. Their activities have direct and indirect impact on the communities in which they operate. The responsibility of a corporation is not limited to what regulations dictate.

Hence, sincerity and effectiveness in the exercise of corporate social responsibility are important in gaining the goodwill of the community. Therefore, board members should also provide effective oversight for corporate social responsibility activities as well.

Companies are obliged to adhere to the legal and regulatory requirements in each jurisdiction. Therefore, having a proper understanding both of the existing situation and of the potential changes is an important input to exercising sound judgment and protecting the company against regulatory risks.

Last but not least, understanding the expectations, priorities, and concerns of shareholders, and investment community shareholders, is the top priority when it comes to meeting their expectations.

MEASURING THE EFFECTIVENESS OF CORPORATE GOVERNANCE

Boards have the basic responsibility of ensuring sustainable improvements in corporate valuations by providing strategic guidance and oversight regarding management decisions, as well as selecting and changing the management whenever necessary. Success can only be achieved on a sustainable basis, if boards behave as a role model for implementing the CRAFTED principles of governance (consistency, responsibility, accountability, fairness, transparency, effectiveness deployed throughout the organization) in their own operations and ensure that the corporation follows these principles in making key decisions.

The board of directors is the most important element in corporate structures. In particular, clear separation of management rights (taking initiative and implementation) and governance rights (guidance, approval, and oversight), is critical in minimizing potential "agency" risks of the management.

Issues such as the composition of boards, their agenda and processes for decision making and how they Learn to continuously improve the governance of the corporation, critically influence both the quality of decisions and of management. The main responsibilities of the board are to provide effective Oversight and strategic Guidance for the management. The quality of their decisions is critically dependent on the quality of the Information they have. Establishing a Culture that sets the right tone at the top is critical for establishing "trust" with all its stakeholders (the "LOGIC" of governance).

The success of the board depends on making sound judgments in numerous situations that involve balancing different interests: risk versus reward, short term versus long term, effective oversight versus motivating management, ethical considerations versus market practices, and competing interests of different stakeholders.

Good corporate governance is very important for sustainable development, not only for the individual company, but also for the economy as a whole. Therefore, the quality of governance should be continuously improved and good governance should be promoted. However, what is not measured, cannot be quantifiably improved. Hence, there is a need for a model to measure the quality of corporate governance.

Most attempts to measure the quality of corporate governance focus on compliance-related issues. Numerous rating models also seem to focus on the inputs of governance, such as the composition of boards and the separation of the CEO and chairman roles. However, they do not pay sufficient attention to the quality of information, decision-making processes, nor link the effectiveness of governance to output measures such as the brand image, employee and customer satisfaction indices, or profitability and value creation. Also, most measures fail to deal with learning and development in governance.

First, what is more important than which demographic characteristics a board member possesses, is what kind of experience he/she has and what types of behavior he/she portrays. Therefore, gender, nationality and age diversity are not sufficient to evaluate the effectiveness of a board. One should also evaluate the relevance of the experience of board members to address the main challenges the company is likely to face.

Second, an important issue is that the quality of the information that the board gets is a key determinant of its effectiveness. Whether relevant and timely information, presented in context, with the benchmarks and alternatives identified, assumptions understood and stress-tested, and whether the potential effects of various alternatives on different stakeholders have been taken into account, has a significant impact on the quality of the board's decision.

Third, the impact of a board's decisions on output measures should be evaluated, not just inputs such as information quality. Governance is important for the sustainability of value creation. If the model that aims to measure effectiveness of governance does not evaluate the linkages to output measures – not only financial performance, but also lead indicators such as customer, employee, or other stakeholder satisfaction – it would be missing an important dimension.

Fourth, boards should also be focusing not only on the business results, but also how business results are obtained. As an outstanding performance could sometimes be due to excessive risk-taking, resulting in a relatively good performance during a particular period, it may not be sustainable. Such an elaborate evaluation of management proposals requires an open and transparent culture, where members are encouraged to challenge assumptions and evaluate alternatives.

Fifth, also, as there is a time lag between a decision and its impact, the board's performance should be evaluated over a period of time, not at a specific time.

Finally, the purpose of measuring the effectiveness of governance should be to improve it continuously. Therefore, assessing how a board learns and invests in developing its own performance should be an important dimension of the model.

Therefore, we have developed a model that tries to remedy these shortcomings. The essence of the ARGE Corporate Governance Model© is to evaluate how the "CRAFTED" principles are applied to the "LOGIC" of governance.

The model aims to incorporate not only structural aspects of governance, such as the composition of the boards, but also behavioral aspects such as the evaluation of a sufficient number of alternatives in decision making, the quality of information that forms the basis of sound judgment, the culture of decision making, the processes, and the results of oversight and guidance functions of the board of directors.

The model also seeks to check whether there is a sound, integrated approach to governance; whether the determined approach is deployed systematically throughout different processes and levels of the organization, whether the approach to governance brings the desired results and that these are benchmarked with the best in class examples, and whether there is a continuous monitoring of results that feeds into learning and improvements.

The evaluation and backbone of the model stands on four main areas, three of which are inputs and the fourth, an output:

- the right people (input);
- the right team (input);
- the right processes (input);
- improvement in business results (output).

The ARGE Corporate Governance Model© provides a set of questions and best practice examples regarding the application of the "LOGIC" of governance to the four dimensions of people, team, processes, and business results.

The model also looks at how continuous improvement processes are implemented in governance mechanisms. The model analyses the people, team, and processes on the basis of corporate governance principles.

A self-assessment guide is developed based on the model. The guide attempts to check the coherence of the structure with the board's conduct and its continuous improvement processes. Questions are prepared to consider whether, in each dimension, a proper tone is set at the top, an effective information provision process is established, and a proper process is in place for appropriate guidance and adequate oversight.

Furthermore, the developments on these issues both over time and in comparison to benchmarks are considered.

Answers to these questions are rated according to **BaSICS** measurement that tries to identify whether there is a **Ba**sic definition against which performance can be measured, that the **S**cope is adequate, **I**mplementation is realized throughout the processes and organization, that there is **C**ontinuous improvement, and an adequate system has been developed and resources deployed for **S**ustainability (see Table 6.3).

SOME RECOMMENDATIONS

There is increasing pressure on boards of directors to perform. They are expected to uphold corporate governance, be strategically creative, and to improve the performance of their companies in an increasingly competitive environment.

Even though boards may be comprised of very experienced members, it is possible they collectively make wrong decisions. It is important to learn from these mistakes. One common mistake is to have overconfidence in the company or the board itself, assuming that the company is among the best run. There are mechanisms to avoid such overconfidence:

- to make scenario analyses to prepare for adverse outcomes;
- to make risk assessment to increase sensitivities to weaknesses identified;
- to make phased decisions to retain strategic flexibility.

Boards, particularly of conglomerates, have a tendency to regard sale or closing down of a business line as a sign of failure and therefore are not always objective enough to exit that business. However, it is important for a board to realize that sometimes the simplest and the best way to create value is to cease activities that no longer represent any value. They should make realistic and independent assessments when considering disposal or closure, even if there were strong supporters or initiators of the business within the board.

Table 6.3 The BaSICS criteria

	Based on definition	Scope	Implementation	Continuous development	Sustainability
C – culture	Values and principles are defined	Values and principles are perpetuated with applications	Values and principles are disseminated throughout the organization	Implementation of values and principles are monitored to identify improvement opportunities	No leniency when values are breached
I – information	Timely updated	Comprehensive (dimensions) and comparable (trends)	Shared and consistent	Best practice benchmarks are considered	Investments are made for information processes and sharing
G – guidance	Based on information and consistent with the mission and principles of the corporation	Comprehensive (dimensions)	Establishing the required communication structure for sharing the strategies and objectives	Decision making with the assessment of various alternatives, results, and risks	Investments are made for incorporate learning into decision-making processes
O – oversight	Defined procedures, principles, and rules exist	Comprehensive (dimensions)	Accountability	Weakness in internal control mechanisms are identified and remedied	Confidence to share with stakeholders
L – learning	Limited examples exist	There are sporadic examples in different dimensions	There are examples that are disseminated throughout the organization	Determining the objective for development	Rewarding learning and development

Similarly for some boards, changing course on an investment decision is harder than it should be. If a bad investment decision is not recognized it may result in "throwing good money after bad" – unnecessarily saddling the corporation. A board of directors that has the courage to recognize a bad decision will ultimately be more successful in adding value to the company.

Even though it is important to prevent unnecessary spending to correct bad decisions, it is equally important to not to be overcautious and stand in the way of innovation. It is helpful to break investments down into stages that will allow for independent interim evaluation and allow for flexibility.

Another common misjudgment by boards is to approach different categories of investment or spending with different criteria. A million dollar marketing error costs the corporation the same as a million dollar production error. Sometimes a more liberal approach to undertaking a new or fashionable line of business can be very costly to the corporation.

To misread market conditions can also prove to be a mistake. Especially in countries where the economic environment is more volatile and moves in booms and busts, wrong assumptions about market conditions can lead to losses for the company.

If for instance a company suffers from high levels of inventory in a recessionary year and follows an overly conservative production policy, it may be unable to meet rising demand in the upturn and lose market share. Therefore, in more volatile environments, it may be more appropriate to focus on the decision horizon and increase flexibility, as this may be more appropriate than annual or multiyear plans.

Intolerance to diversity of ideas and rewarding conformity to team opinion also presents a risk to the company. In a board where everybody is of the same opinion, there is no need for more than one member! An environment conducive to debate of different points of view will encourage creative thinking and therefore enable the company to take advantage of opportunities and recognize risks.

CONSTRUCTIVE CRITICAL THINKING

It is very important that board members establish a system of constructive critical thinking to generate effective strategic deliberation. We cannot expect a board to be successful if all the members accept every proposal presented to them without a critical evaluation.

Critical thinking is challenging all assumptions, information and judgments, and evaluating different aspects of issues at hand before coming to a conclusion. Critical thinking involves making judgments about the relevance, significance, fairness, and logic of the issue at hand.

There are different dimensions to critical thinking. The first step is to be able to identify the relevant dimensions, assign weights to each dimension, identify which ones will have significance for the results, and to live with uncertainty about those which are not critical.

The second step is to determine whether we have enough information to deal with the issue at hand, and if not, how to overcome this lack of information, and to raise questions to secure the gaps.

The third step is to have knowledge about theoretical models and being able to judge the information with respect to such models.

The fourth step is to make sure that everybody understands the assumptions and theoretical underpinnings of models presented. Otherwise, there may be gaps in understanding among the board members, an across the board understanding of concepts and assumptions is important in critical thinking.

The fifth step is to be able to make inferences and check information presented for consistency. This also enables further access to information.

The sixth step is to be able to concur on objective criteria to judge alternatives. If there is no consensus on evaluation criteria, then it is not possible to reach consensus for a decision.

The seventh step is to be able to judge the strength, depth, and breadth of justifications for a decision. It is an important part of critical thinking to determine whether assumptions or justifications are sufficient for a decision.

People with critical thinking skills have some common characteristics. One of these is their systematic thinking and work discipline. They are flexible and open to new ideas and change. Another important characteristic is perseverance with respect to their undertakings.

People with critical thinking skills are open-minded in considering alternative perspectives, recognizing and assessing their assumptions, implications, and practical consequences. A board member who does not have the self-confidence to accept that personal views and approach can be challenged by another member cannot function effectively and has a negative effect on the general atmosphere of board meetings.

Finally, critical thinkers are hard workers, and can communicate effectively in reaching solutions to difficult issues. A board member who is not well prepared before a meeting is not exercising the discipline required for critical thinking, nor can he win the trust of fellow board members.

Absence of critical thinking on the board results in unhealthy decisions. Therefore, one of the key responsibilities of the chairperson of the board is to have a diverse board that will approach issues differently, encourage critical thinking, and create an environment conducive to challenge.

MANAGEMENT CULTURE IS MORE IMPORTANT THAN MANAGEMENT STRUCTURE

Establishing the right structural and procedural elements are given a lot of emphasis. Yet corporate culture is more important in setting the tone for good governance. The most striking example in recent history is the example of Enron, which seemed to have a lot of the right management infrastructures in place, as indicated by its high rating.

Corporate culture is the cornerstone of creating trust inside and outside the company. The implementation of consistency, responsibility, accountability, fairness, transparency, and effectiveness deployed "CRAFTED" throughout the organization becomes paramount.

EXAMPLES OF BEHAVIORS EXPECTED FROM AN ORGANIZATION WITH GOOD GOVERNANCE

1. Management should not benefit personally from the company's activities or assets, except from their stipulated compensation and reward packages.
2. There should be no transactions with the company or its affiliates that is not in line with market prices or practices.
3. The management should not assume too much risk on behalf of the shareholders with the purpose of inflating short-term performance of the company.
4. The management should not use company resources to build an empire for themselves.
5. There should be no tendency toward nepotism. Qualifications of the individuals should be the only criteria in selecting and promoting them.
6. Mechanisms should be in place to prevent insider trading.
7. There should be no impediments to effective functioning of internal control systems.
8. Management should assume responsibility that all employees are adequately informed and trained to prevent conflicts of interest within the organization.
9. Management should assume responsibility that all employees observe all legal and ethical stipulations, and that there is an effective whistle blowing mechanism to identify violations.
10. The independence of external auditors should not be compromised by giving them too many other assignments.
11. There should be a competitive compensation system to ensure that competent individuals with the right qualifications are attracted to the company and rewarded for performance.
12. No shareholder should be given preferential treatment, and commercial transactions made with shareholders should be carried out on an arm's length basis.
13. Unethical conduct such as bribery should be a cause for dismissal.
14. Management should behave fairly toward all stakeholders such as employees, suppliers, and distributors.

15. Overconfidence in internal capabilities has to be avoided, in order to be able to utilize third party resources for improving company performance.
16. Cutbacks in investments should be evaluated carefully to avoid threats to the company's future. Particularly, investments in intangibles such as the brand should be watched carefully, since damage in the short term is difficult to measure.
17. Continuous improvement and benchmarking with best practice examples should be encouraged.
18. Public disclosure requirements about developments that may have an effect on the value of the company must be strictly observed.
19. Systematic assessment should be conducted of risks and opportunities concerning the company's future.
20. Corporate social responsibility toward society and future generations should be taken seriously.

ETHICAL VALUES AS A FOUNDATION FOR BUILDING TRUST

The most important expectation from a board is the responsibility for stewardship and the duty of care, which involves ensuring compliance throughout the organization with ethical rules above and beyond laws and regulations. This emphasis on ethical values becomes more and more important in the post economic crisis world, when organizations, particularly in the financial sector, need to reestablish their credibility.

Ethical values may differ slightly between countries depending on societal expectations. However, it is possible to summarize common global ethical values under the following headings:

Corporate social responsibility – a corporation is expected to contribute voluntarily to ensure a better environment and society. The expectation that it will respect human rights, institute healthy and safe working conditions, protect the environment, avoid being part of corruption, and meet international standards is not limited to the corporation's own organization, but extends to its business partners as well.

Fair investigation – a corporation is expected to be open and fair in sharing information and documents when it or its management is faced with any legal allegations, and not to attempt to hide or destroy any information. The biggest blow to Arthur Andersen during the Enron incident came from demonstrating insufficient sensitivity on this issue.

The responsibility to protect the environment – a corporation is expected to respect the environment and take care not to cause damage to the environment through its activities or the activities of its business partners. Outsourcing certain activities does relieve the company of its responsibilities in this respect.

No misrepresentation in public disclosures – a corporation's business results must be shared in a transparent manner. Not sharing or misrepresenting information is unacceptable.

Effectiveness of internal controls – senior management of a corporation is responsible for the effectiveness of internal controls to ensure that the employees observe ethical standards. This responsibility extends to agreements made with third parties, guarantees of company's products and services, and financial transactions.

Consumer protection – knowingly manufacturing products or rendering services that may harm or mislead its customers constitutes a blatant violation of ethical values.

Unfair or deceptive competition – marketing practices such as forcing unwanted products along with wanted ones, pressuring customers to sign exclusivity agreements, and employing out-of-market pricing policies in order to force out competition are unacceptable. Obvious transgressions in these areas may in fact be penalized by competition laws.

Preventing the exposure of unethical behavior – if and when unethical behavior is discovered within an organization, the corporation must not prevent investigation by public prosecutors, and it must not protect those who exhibit unethical behavior.

The responsibility of the board – the board is responsible for the integrity of the corporation's public disclosures and for protecting the rights of its shareholders as a whole.

Care must be taken to establish systems along these principles, but also to have board members that have this understanding. Compliance with ethical standards is important in earning the trust of the community; local and global. Earning this trust creates value for the company.

Trust is hard to earn, easy to lose. Keeping hard-earned trust is a dynamic process that requires maintenance. Inherent in this process is keeping up with a constantly changing world. Therefore, believing in change and being proactive for change becomes a prerequisite for earning and maintaining trust.

COMMON MANAGEMENT CHALLENGES

Board members should also be aware of the challenges for the company and the management and continually assess the capability of the management to handle these challenges. Some common issues faced by numerous companies are:

The Need for Change

Always desiring the better is a fundamental human attribute. The drive to search for better is at the foundation of development and progress. This is true for companies as well as individuals.

This points to a need for constant change, because a service or product that was "above standard" yesterday is "standard" when we are used to it and "substandard" when we find a better service or product. In competitive environments, those that cannot manage change find themselves changed.

Developments in technology have increased the rate of change and the rate at which the change reaches end users. Therefore, organizations also have to increase the rate at which they can implement and manage change. This makes managing change an important attribute of current day leaders.

Comparison of company results with best practice examples is an effective way of achieving consensus within the organization for the need and urgency of change. This is why it is important to have the comparison process as part of the corporate culture.

Believing in Change

Believing in the need for change is critical for achieving it. Success is the best agent for spreading the belief. Therefore, when the change process is being planned, it is as important to plan for short-term results as it is long-term results. The short-term gains should also be communicated well to increase the momentum of the process.

The first step in implementing change is establishing a coalition that demonstrates its belief in the process by its actions. This coalition that champions the change should include members from all segments of the organization – from the board to the factory worker. It is particularly important to include respected individuals in the group in order to facilitate an ownership of the process at all levels. The champions for change should also have the powers to ensure implementation.

The information and performance evaluation systems within the organization should also be restructured to support the new system to motivate management and employees. This is also important to inform information–based decision-making processes.

It is critical to be able to lead change. Only strong leaders can focus companies on ambitious targets. Leaders of change are capable of self-evaluation, target constant improvement, value human resource, and adopt learning, transparency, communication, and sharing as a philosophy of life. They set an example by demonstrating the foregoing characteristics in their actions.

Institutions should support change leaders at all levels. Change is the basis for improvement, and therefore life itself.

Quality in Management

It is as important to have a roadmap for change as it is to understand the importance of change. Companies that strive for quality as a philosophy of management successfully determine the need for, and achieve change.

The concept of quality is generally associated with an adherence to certain standards, and of being developed. However, the concept of quality that we discuss here goes beyond that, to be defined as surpassing expectations. Inherent in this definition is the aspiration of mankind to constantly reach for the better. It is a dynamic concept, since every time expectations are met the desire to improve moves the process on again.

A product or service that is of high quality to its consumer today will no longer meet expectations tomorrow. Therefore we have to be constantly aware of the need to surpass ourselves to provide a quality product or service.

The concept of quality goes back a long time in history. Phoenicians held the right "to cut off the hand of those who do not task well." In the organized brotherhood of Akhism in Anatolia, trade guilds practiced a form of self-supervision where they used to hang the shoe of the under-quality producer from the roof, indicating it off limits for trade for a period of time.

The penalty for lack of quality in today's world is less drastic: loss of market share.

How Can We Achieve Quality?

Management quality is best achieved by applying certain principles. The role of leadership and its congruence with objectives is critical in the process. The most effective leadership is not established with power but with gaining over minds and hearts. To achieve this, the leader must be able to set the objectives very clearly, and demonstrate a commitment to the objectives by his decisions and actions. Consistency of word and deed is critical for a leader.

Being customer focused is a major advantage for a company. Measuring performance by the value added makes a company more productive, and more attractive to its customers. If the customer is made to pay for an activity that does not generate value, a recipe for failure is formulated.

One of the important vehicles for improving management quality is managing by processes and inputs. Identifying processes that create value, organizing the company based on these processes, establishing performance criteria and measuring performance on a regular basis all serve to increase motivation. Performance that is not measured in some way is generally not improved.

Sharing performance information with employees, developing their skills, and empowering them all add to constant improvement of performance. People that carry out their work with full commitment are the guarantee of strong performance.

In today's world, companies are dependent on outside suppliers for their products and services. Therefore, it becomes critical to manage not only our own company, but the entire value chain. An organization demonstrates its management quality not only by its internal relationships, but also by its relationships with its various partners. The real competition is not with our suppliers or sales outlets, but with other value chains. The chain is only as strong as its weakest link, and no one is as strong as the complete chain.

The focus should not solely be on turnover, but on value created. The highest value added will result from continuous development, innovation, and differentiation.

Corporate social responsibility is another important aspect of the high management quality of an organization. Companies that embrace their social responsibilities gain also by improving their own internal management skills and by increasing their mind share with their customers.

In summary, quality is a philosophy of life. Applying these principles in a consistent manner will increase management quality. Increasing management quality is the most effective way of increasing our prosperity. We should therefore have a good grasp of the quality concept, and assume responsibility for increasing management quality in private, public, and civil society institutions. Spreading the quality concept by living by it is a gift to our future generations.

Vision and Strategic Outlook

Success is sustainable value creation. Sustainability in value creation requires not only "doing the right things" (strategy) and "doing things right" (total quality management), but also having the right structure and culture (good governance). Strategy comes from the Greek word *strategos*, which derives from two ancient Greek words, *stratos* (army) and *ago* (lead).

The essence of strategy is to make consistent choices on which demand (potential or strategic) to fulfill, and how. What differentiates a company is its mission, vision, and the strategy it follows to reach them. In short, strategic thinking is the ability to differentiate in a consistent manner. Companies that have a clear mission, vision, and strategy benefit from (i) focusing their resources, whether physical or mental, and avoid activities that do not create value, (ii) a better balance between short-term and long-term goals, (iii) having a tool for team building and the motivation for more effective resource utilization, and (iv) an ability to capture value creation opportunities faster.

Characteristics of an Effective Vision

- Vividly imaginable: provides a picture of success for the future.
- Desirable: responds to expectations of all stakeholders.
- Stretched yet realistic: sets a goal that is feasible to achieve with hard work.
- Focused: clear enough to provide guidance in decision making.
- Flexible: easy to adapt to changing conditions and different dimensions.
- Easy to communicate: so that all employees can understand and internalize it.

Effective communication of the mission and the vision of the company also improve the effectiveness of their implementation and therefore require special attention. For effective communication, a vision statement should:

i. be written in straightforward language;
ii. be easy to understand and remember;
iii. be enriched by examples and stories for ease of recall;
iv. be communicated consistently through different media to increase mind share;
v. have linkages between the key decisions and the vision provided;
vi. be backed by leaders who practice what they preach;
vii. be able to receive feedback, in order for two-way communication to produce enrichment.

Setting the strategy is an analytically oriented art. A good strategy is like a compass. It helps in guiding the company through the difficulties of the marketplace. A good strategy benefits from the effectiveness of the development process, and from the consistency of the leader.

Adhering to certain principles increases the success rate of a good strategy:

1. **Fit between strategy and resources** – the strategy should be in congruence with the organization's competencies, structure, culture, reward mechanisms, and processes, and with the resources it can mobilize.
2. **Clarity of focus** – one of the key aspects of strategy is making a choice. Therefore, identifying what not to do is just as important as identifying what to do.
3. **Dynamic** – a strategic plan should take into account the potential responses of all parties, competitors, suppliers, customers, and so on, and should include contingency plans for the expected responses of the various parties.
4. **Holistic** – the implications of implementing the strategy for all of the key functions should be thought out.

Internalizing the strategy within the institution requires certain steps:

1. **Communicating the vision to all stakeholders** – actions of the stakeholders will be consistent with the strategy to the extent that it is understood by them.
2. **Making the organizational structure consistent with strategy.**
3. **Training** – without the required information or skills, people will not feel empowered.
4. **Making human resources and information technology systems consistent with strategy** – to be able to follow whether implementation is consistent with strategy, and to establish the right incentives, it is critically important for infrastructure to be in place.

In short, strategy is at the basis of a company's success, and it is a management approach that requires quality thinking, effective communication, and disciplined execution.

Risk Management

We have lived through a period that showed financial companies can fail at risk management. It is clear there is no profit without risk. However, taking risk and taking advantage of risk management practices are different issues. Taking risk without managing risk is gambling.

Good risk management requires correct identification of the potential risks. Categorizing risks helps prevent overlooking some areas of risk. A company should identify risks in inputs, manufacturing processes, market conditions, financial markets, legal, and regulatory environment. *A survey by Deloitte after the crisis found that too few boards had actually defined the risk parameters well.*

A second step is assigning probabilities to the risks materializing and evaluating the potential costs to the company, and determining the precautions. For high impact risks, risk mitigation measures such as insurance or different financing models such as leasing can be employed. Different methods can be used for different types of risks.

In the case of financial institutions, hedging techniques can be employed. However, using judgment is as important as the numbers. One of the reasons that JPMorgan Chase & Co fared better in the financial crisis was because they applied a more conservative approach to risk mitigation and Jamie Dimon's good grasp of the financial risks involved. In retrospect, there were several instances of the bank cutting down credit lines to special investment vehicles, accurately estimating the potential outcomes, and paying close attention to risk diversification. The difference in assessment of hedges between many others and JPMorgan Chase & Co is also instructive. While numerous banks proved to have "hedged and forgot," paying no attention to inherent tail risks, JPMorgan Chase & Co calculated its risks on the basis of whether hedges would hold or would prove worthless.

In the period building up to the crisis, there was a growing reliance on complicated models built up by PhDs in mathematics. Complexity of products made a thorough due diligence next to impossible, resulting in inherent risks being opaque to many investors or boards alike. The principles to be taken into account in risk management are summarized below:

1. The main factor in risk management is not the technique employed but rather the experience and grasp of those who are evaluating it.
2. Business models should pay particular attention to risk diversification.
3. Transparency in management and information is critical in mitigating risks.

4. It is important to consider what is known and what is unknown. It must be remembered that all techniques and models are built on assumptions.
5. A disciplined approach should be taken to apply controls and audit mechanisms. We see that business managers employed many tactics to undermine the authority of risk managers.
6. Risks and rewards should be properly measured to determine which businesses or assets generate adequate risk adjusted returns.

Uncertainty Management

Uncertainty is a fact of life. It is possible to manage uncertainty rather than seeing it as a source of stress.

There are four categories of uncertainty from a management point of view: distinct variables, foreseeable uncertainty, unforeseeable uncertainty, and chaos.

Different vehicles can be employed in the management of these four categories of risk. Taking the right decisions requires taking into account how the world will be as much as how the world is. Therefore understanding the uncertainty well forms the basis of right decision making. Variability due to a number of small effects that are difficult to control is generally managed using statistical control methods. Therefore, the impacts and limits can be determined by sensitivity analyses, and provisioning can be made. As an example, keeping work in process inventories can be used as a precautionary measure for variables affecting production.

Removing the root causes of such variables by identifying them through use of statistical methods reduces the need for provisional resources and increases productivity.

The second type of uncertainty is where potential outcomes are known, but not the probability of their occurrence. Foreseeable uncertainty requires managers to take precautions using decision trees to determine potential outcomes. Management can then identify contingency plans to be implemented under different outcomes, and can also devise strategies to influence the probability of occurrence of certain outcomes. If these plans are prepared in conjunction with business partners, response times can be faster to manage foreseeable certainties.

In the third type of uncertainty, given that the possible outcomes are too numerous to model into decision trees, scenario analyses can be employed to arrive at possible responses. The analysis is designed to allow improved decision making by allowing the consideration of outcomes and their implications. Scenarios are prepared for certain "typical" outcomes, and risk mitigation strategies for these cases are discussed within the management team for mental preparation.

Chaos is generally a temporary type of uncertainty. Risks are very high in these periods and those with sufficient resources can make the choices to shape the future. In the aftermath of the recent economic crisis, P&G is launching its biggest expansion and opening 19 factories around the world and investing heavily in new ideas, as are Intel and IBM.

Other players make the minimum investments required to weather the storm and keep their options open, or take the opportunity to reposition themselves. Managing uncertainty requires reading it correctly and using the right tools to deal with it.

STRATEGY AND SIMULATION MODELS

In this day and age, the road to success goes through well-informed decision making and fast execution. Wrong or slow decisions can have high costs for companies. In an increasingly complicated environment, there is a need to employ methods to increase the effectiveness of right decision making.

Research shows that after one week, people can only remember 15% of what they have learned in a classroom. Case studies on the other hand, increase both the amount of content remembered, and the length of time that it is remembered. As child educators know, an effective way to learn can be through role play. This is why simulation models are gaining more popularity in executive training programs.

Learning from mistakes is another way of learning effectively, but these can be very costly for companies. Employing simulation models allows top management to evaluate alternatives without suffering costs.

Speed of strategic decisions is important in an age where product evolution is very fast. Simulation models enable information building in days, where such information could be obtained through a few cycles in the market, taking a longer time.

Simulation models are also used to test how the strategy stands up against possible reactions of competitors. This enables formulating strategies with lower risk profiles.

Simulations also facilitate a clearer understanding by management of the impact of their decisions on the business and value of the company.

Once the model is established, it becomes easy to train various parts of the company regarding the impact of the decisions of their own departments on other parts of the company and the results. This improves the quality of decision making.

Perhaps most importantly, simulation models force management to look at the business through the eyes of their competitors. Management has a better chance at evaluating their competitors' strategic movements if they understand them.

The "just-in-time" concept is important for training as well, a prompt opportunity of practical application of new learning reinforces the training. Simulation models also allow for this with strategy training, where practical application is more difficult.

STRATEGIC SCENARIOS

Uncertainty in the behavior of existing or potential competitors or of the future in general makes strategic planning difficult. For this reason, several institutions use scenario analyses for strategy building. American think-tank RAND Corporation started using scenario analyses back after World War II.

Strategic planning through scenarios stimulates creative thinking. In general, the strategic planning teams in institutions are made up of people that have similar approaches to the business model. It is generally expected that people senior enough to generate strategic plans have worked with the institution for several years. However, it is also true that people that have worked in the same environment have a similar experience base, and therefore fewer differences in their approach. For this reason, some institutions include people from the outside or new people in the company with a different background in their strategy development process. Scenario analyses instigate creativity because uncertainties or opinion differences can be modeled into scenarios.

Scenario analyses test the flexibility and adequacy of the adopted strategies in the face of possible future scenarios. This facilitates identification and awareness of the indicators that lead to breaking points. Resource planning can thus be made for reducing risks associated with strategies.

Scenario analyses also enable realistic alternative plans to be developed, and facilitate speedier adaptation of the institution to changing conditions. Knowing what steps to take under different conditions enriches the strategic thinking.

Scenario analyses speed up the corporate learning process. Identifying the strengths and weaknesses of the institution, and the threats and opportunities under different future scenarios contributes to gaining insight without bearing actual costs of living through them.

More and more institutions are using scenario analyses because institutions with mental preparation have a chance to influence the turn of events rather than react to them. The road to success includes being prepared for the future.

CUSTOMER FOCUSED ORGANIZATION

As developments in technology facilitate information sharing, companies in the same sector have access to and benefit from similar technologies, ways of doing business, and skill sets. In such an environment, differentiating the company from among its competitors becomes more and more difficult. The simplest way to determine why customers prefer one product or service over another is to ask them. Thus, increasing customer satisfaction by meeting their expectations in various processes will put the company at an advantage.

Trying to reach all customers in the marketplace with the same package of benefits or with the same methods entails the assumption that all their expectations are the same. However, whether individuals or companies, every customer has different expectations owing to their specific circumstances. Moreover, these expectations are not static, but changing with changing needs, or with different alternatives available to them in the market. Therefore, customer preferences are dynamic.

Rather than "formulating" a package of benefits and trying to convince customers to prefer the package, companies should get to know their customers well, understand what their needs and preferences are, and then aim to meet their expectations. This will enable a company not only to increase its market share, but also to use its resources most effectively.

Given limited resources, it is not possible to meet the specific product or service needs of each customer. Therefore, the best solution is to categorize customers in groups that are as homogeneous as possible, and focus design and marketing processes based on the expectations of these groups.

Market segmentation is the process of dividing a total market into market groups consisting of people who have relatively similar product needs and buying behaviors. A market segment consists of individuals, groups or organizations with one or more characteristics that cause them to have relatively similar product needs.

Marketing departments of companies should constantly be on the lookout to identify niche products or services that more precisely match the needs of customers in a selected market segment.

Customer segmentation is a three step process. The first step is to determine a certain number of segments depending on segmentation variables and criteria. The next step is to determine one or more groups for marketing. Since it is generally not possible to reach all customer segments, strategic choices have to be made taking into account competitive opportunities, company objectives, customer needs, and the company's financial and technical resources. This analysis should lead to the last step of identifying a niche market for the company. Segments where competitors are not active, or where marketing advantages can be created can be developed by bringing new approaches.

The segmentation process forms the basis of marketing plans and facilitates the following.

Simpler marketing process – the requirements of a homogeneous group will not show wide variation making it easier to meet their expectations. It becomes possible to design products specific to those expectations. The needs can be classified under a few distinct headings, the message or the benefit to the customer can be clearly stated to meet these needs, and it is simpler to differentiate the company from competitors. The company looks stronger to its existing or potential customer base.

Identifying niche markets – if there are segments of the market that are not served, or served well, competition will be less in these segments. Therefore, introducing or improving products or services to these segments makes it relatively easy to gain market share.

Increasing productivity – focusing on the right segments for the company enables the most productive use of marketing resources. Customer segmentation prevents wrong messages or messages to the wrong customer, and facilitates development of more effective and less costly marketing campaigns.

If we offer the same service or product to all customers, we will meet the expectations of very few. The benefits of the product to the customer are more important to him than the specific features of the product. Therefore it is important to differentiate designs, processes, and services with this in mind.

LOYAL CUSTOMER OR PROFITABLE CUSTOMER?

Measuring and developing customer loyalty is gaining importance in Total Quality Management (TQM). Studies show that it is more productive to keep existing customers than it is to add new ones.

However, this does not imply that loyal customers are necessarily profitable customers. Therefore, conducting customer profitability analyses and employing policies that will be attractive to profitable customers can be a determinant in a company's success. As more and more companies are using the customer relations management (CRM) concept, they should take care to include an emphasis on customer profitability.

Improving customer relations is a criterion of success for companies in general. However, a surprising number of companies do not adequately concern themselves with customer profitability. As a result, CRM efforts focus on improving customer satisfaction, without necessarily focusing on profitable customers. While improving customer relations is very important, not differentiating in their favor may lose us some profitable customers.

There are a few reasons why focusing on customer loyalty alone is not sufficient for profitability. Long-term customers demand special care. This is particularly true in relations between a main industry and its side industries. Companies generally cannot reflect the costs of investments they undertake for their loyal customers to their prices. When these types of investments overtake those undertaken to attract new customers, loyal customers become the unprofitable ones.

Loyal customers can also negatively impact profitability through their price negotiations when they realize how important they are to the company, or when they understand the cost structure well. A lot of companies make the mistake of defining loyal customers by the frequency of their purchases, when seasonality can also play a role in timing of purchases.

Another common criterion is the size of the purchases. It must be remembered however that the buyers of sizable quantities know the market and alternatives very well and may be the buyers of the company products with the smallest profit margins. This criterion may result in profitability losses particularly with companies that do not reflect logistics costs to their prices.

Therefore making the right profitability analysis is very important. A customer profitability analysis should take into account not only the product costs but also the activities necessary to serve certain customers. Only after we calculate the profitability right should we focus on improving customer relations. These may in fact be loyal, new, or one time customers.

Another problem that needs to be addressed is how to make an unprofitable loyal customer into a profitable one, or if that is not possible, how to exit that relationship. A lot of companies end up suffering because they cannot make the decision to exit unprofitable relationships.

SECURING MIND SHARE: PR, COMMUNICATIONS, AND R&D

The world is getting smaller with developments in information and communication technologies and logistic systems. It is possible for companies to reach clients in different markets. As new product developments gain pace, customers get bombarded with more information and their ability to choose widens, impressing customers becomes more difficult and more important.

Success requires on the one hand identifying new needs and developing the products to meet those needs, and on the other hand, making sure that the value that is created is widely and correctly communicated.

Therefore, Public Relations (PR) and communication expenses should not be treated as expense items alone, but rather as important corporate investments. To treat PR and communication as a corporate investment means setting aside adequate funds and evaluating the spending and results as carefully as we would any other investment budget.

For good communication, we have to first have the product or service that creates value. To create the value, a company has to be constantly on the alert with its research and development activity. Companies that cut back on their research and development activity are cutting back on their future.

Determining the target audience is another important aspect of good communication. The characteristics of the target audience determine both the message and the medium to be employed.

Using the KISS "keep it simple, stupid" principle enables easy comprehension of the message by large numbers of people. The message should be packaged to attract interest, as well as include a dimension of differentiation of the product.

A convincing and distinguishing message can focus on any one or more of the following: (1) what need the product or service is intended to serve, (2) how it will be used, (3) what effects it will have when used, (4) benefits proven by research, and (5) information on hard to replicate or attractive production methods (vis-à-vis the environment for example).

Media is only one of the vehicles of communicating with the customer. Customer's experience with the product, its packaging, sales points, experience in case of direct contact, and other customer's opinions are also important ways of communication with the customer and should be used effectively.

It is difficult to measure the impact of communication. However, we should spend time and resource to measure this impact because we cannot improve what we cannot measure.

Increasing the mind share in society is not only a function of communication. Corporate behavior is as critical as corporate discourse in good communication. In an age where people are under constant bombardment of information, companies with corporate social responsibility that contribute to solutions of social issues increase their mind share.

An indicator of development of a country is the recognition they have among another country's citizens. This is why more and more multinationals from Korea to Finland are paying special attention to establishing lasting relationships with their customer base. In this way, they are not only successfully marketing their current products, but are investing in the competitive advantages of their future.

To speed up the pace of our development and make it last, we must increase our mind share in current and potential markets. This is the reason why we should not undermine the importance of PR, communication, and research and development.

CREATING A BRAND

"Nothing is valuable on its own. The worth of anything is attributed to it by others." These words of John Barth point to the importance of brand value that companies create in the minds of people.

In the new economy, the success of managers is determined more by the value they create than by their profitability management. To be successful in creating value, identifying new needs and creating business models to meet them on the one hand, and ensuring correct and widespread perception of company values on the other hand becomes critical. The value reached by correct management of this company perception is called corporate brand value.

The fact that companies like Coca-Cola, Nike, or GE have market values that are greater than can be explained by their assets or annual profits is not only a function of their good performance but also of the importance they place on increasing their corporate brand value.

Companies that have a successful brand can carry out their marketing activities more economically than their competitors, have more negotiation power with their distribution channels, are more successful in getting new customers or offering new products, and can fight off threats from competitors without loss of market share. The lead time in fighting off competition is probably the biggest gain in a world where timing is the most important competitive element.

Corporate brand is a concept beyond product brand, product marketing, or product launch. It is created and managed by a planned and disciplined approach. It is a task not entrusted to marketing teams but to be undertaken by top management. Creating a brand is managing not only the marketing, PR, and advertisement functions, but all functions of the company with a specific intent.

GROWTH AND PROFITABILITY

Growth and increasing profitability is at the top of the agenda for all companies. Growth is achieved with the understanding that every step taken is one of several on a long journey.

Growth is possible in any sector, in any geographical location, and at any stage of the business. Growth requires changes in strategic approach, organizational structures, and work processes. Since limiting factors are company specific, there is no single recipe for growth. What is important is to identify a growth strategy that takes into account all the infrastructural elements of growth.

Process improvements should cover all processes starting from procurement to the product reaching the customer, and should aim to improve productivity as well as to remove factors limiting growth.

Important elements of the costs of goods sold are dependent on factors outside the company. Therefore supply chain management improvements are important contributors to growing sales and profitability.

Other important cost elements in production depend on decisions made at investment stage and on product design. This means the planning stage is critical for future growth. The thought and planning stage should be extensive, and the investment stage flexible, and modular.

Investments into distribution channels, marketing and the brand are also important expense items that are part of the infrastructure for growth. As an example of considerations here, formulating a brand name that is difficult to pronounce in international markets makes it more expensive or may constrict its growth phase.

The organizational structure should be clear to prevent internal conflict. Organizational structures where authority delegation prevents timely decision making and implementation are big impediments to growth. Growth phase companies should take care to have simple structures that facilitate speedy decision making.

Organizational structure encompasses all the systems of human resource management. Performance management, incentives, training and development should all be supportive of growth. If for example a company is planning to go into the Russian market as part of its growth plan, an employee or employees that have full grasp of the company corporate culture should be developed in terms of their Russian language abilities.

One of the important triggers of growth is strategic innovation. Therefore, knowing the customer base and their growth and development plans is important. The company should know which sector it positions itself in. When the CEO of Rolex was asked how the market for watches was, his response was, "I would not know, we are in the jewelry business, and not in watches."

Complementing the brand with other products, enhancing the existing products on offer, developing new production capacity and/or mergers and acquisitions are all part of potential growth plans that require resource investment.

When formulating strategy, one of the important decisions to be made is geographical diversity. Which countries to operate in, the critical success factors for that particular location, potential synergies should be evaluated to arrive at product and target customer selections. The strategies for communication, marketing, and branding should follow based on these evaluations.

GEOGRAPHIC EXPANSION AND MERGERS

If we take the case of Turkiye, there are several large markets in its vicinity. Since these countries are still in developmental stages, company valuations are still low. Turkiye has been taking advantage of both cultural affinities as well as its knowledge of the transformation stages through which these economies are passing. This gives Turkish companies a growth potential in markets that are not yet dominated by global giants.

One of the parameters of company valuation is the number of customers served. In a world where those that cannot grow their economic spheres of influence are condemned to disappear, geographical expansion requires a multipronged approach. Governments should also be supportive of the private sector with incentives in identifying certain markets as growth markets.

Developments in information and communication technology, liberalization of trade policies, ease of transportation are all breaking down borders for global business. Scale economies on the other hand, are being redefined. Production facilities are getting smaller as a result of technological developments, yet information resources, technology development, brand, image, and distribution channel economies are getting larger.

Excess production capacity in several sectors is consolidating in the hands of those companies that have successfully achieved scale economies. From telecoms to iron and steel, it is more important to own brands, distribution channels, and research and development capability than it is to own the largest production facilities.

MERGERS AND ACQUISITIONS: DOES SIZE MATTER?

Company size providing competitive advantage is generally explained by scale economies. Scale economies provide a competitive advantage in large production facilities where technology reduces unit costs. In less technology intensive sectors such as ready-made wear, scale does not necessarily increase profitability.

Scale economies are not necessarily relevant only for production facilities. Companies like Walmart use their scale of purchases as a competitive advantage in their negotiations with their suppliers. In a sector where profit margins are small, this negotiating advantage results in significant profitability.

Developing technologies do reduce the scale advantage in production. Yet investments into research and development, brand, and distribution channels still require certain turnover hurdles for profitability regardless of the number of production centers. This is particularly true of industries such as pharmaceuticals where research and development costs are high, but is also true in other industries such as automotive.

A fast moving good company that does not advertize on national television finds it difficult to establish a brand, and cannot obtain adequate margins even if it has cost advantages in production.

Company size provides advantage in scope economies. Operating in more points of the value chain created for the customer may provide a competitive advantage as well. An example is the Koc Group of Turkiye that is the largest producer of white and brown goods as well as automotive. The group has established a consumer finance company that gives an advantage to its production companies.

However, care should be taken to evaluate the pluses and minuses of scope economies. Losing the goodwill of other viable partners in the sector may prove costly. There are companies that have suffered losses by going into sectors for the sake of scope economies where they are not capable.

Another area of size providing advantage is net economies. Microsoft setting standards in operating systems have given them a significant competitive advantage over Apple whose just as good operating systems have lagged due to less widespread licensing. Similarly, the electronic auction company eBay has secured an important competitive advantage in its technological infrastructure by its variety of product and number of participants as a result of being the leader in this area. In Turkiye, the cell phone company Turkcell is still benefiting in terms of profitability and number of users from being the first in the sector.

Company size can meaningfully provide competitive advantage if supported by a strategic outlook. Size for the sake of size does not necessarily provide a competitive advantage.

Companies can achieve global strategic advantages through mergers or acquisitions. Given the dependence on international financial markets for financing these transactions, corporate governance once again comes to the fore.

MULTIPLE MANAGEMENT CENTERS

Economic crises are also instrumental in companies realizing the importance of reaching some sort of global dimension. This may be through establishing operations in other countries or relying on export markets. However, reaching global dimensions requires renewed management approaches as well.

As geographical diversity increases, companies need to revisit their management approaches, as well as concentrating their activities on their core businesses. This requires successful companies to establish long-term outsourcing partnerships with other companies.

Doing business with a strategic partnership approach with both customers and suppliers establishes a company as an indispensable part of many value chains, providing the basis for sustainable competitive advantage and profitability. A true strategic partnership involves a substantial amount of information sharing, transparency, and trust gained over time. Sensitivity to one another's requirements and regular and thorough communication facilitates a lasting strategic partnership.

Managing an effective strategic partnership network requires the company culture to be open to learning, technology, intensive communication, and fast execution. Being open minded and open to sharing form the basis for learning. Companies that aim to make this understanding part of the corporate culture emphasize prompt training compatible with strategy.

Managing the strategic partnership network requires the managers at various points of the chain to have decision making powers. Empowering managers who are close to the market, customer, or the strategic partner facilitates mutual trust and responsiveness. For the entire system to be in congruence, internal communication has to be intensive and thorough as well.

Traditionally, multinational companies apply their own standard business practices whichever market they are in. With their new management approach, globally active companies are now using their home-grown knowledge and execution capability base to bring different solutions to different markets. They view each market not as a sales point for their usual product or service, but as a learning and development opportunity.

This understanding requires multiple management centers rather than a stand-alone head office. Communication and execution speed are critical success factors. Traditional structures where information flow and decision-making happen in a single center do not have the required agility and responsiveness. Moreover, since mutual dependence brings about mutual responsiveness, learning and communication is also faster in companies with multiple management centers.

Another advantage of multiple management centers is that the head office organization, which is relatively removed from the market, is also smaller and more efficient. The CEO and his team are more attuned to their strategic partners, markets, and developments at various points of their organization.

The travel schedules of management of multicentered companies are also multicentered. Therefore their grasp of other markets and developments is easier. Communication based on such a grasp and understanding is more productive, regardless of whether it is in person or through technology.

THE FAST-ACTING COMPANY

The importance of the efficient use of time is best coined in the term "time is cash." A lot of managers are afraid of speedy decision making or action. They worry that "haste makes waste," and results in loss of control. However, speed does not increase but reduces risk or cost, and increases quality. It prevents falling behind in production technologies, and enables timely response to client expectations.

Fast companies can bring new products to market earlier than their competitors. The shorter the time between product design and marketing, the easier it is to reflect customer expectations to the product, and the more current the product. The shorter the time to completion of an investment, the more production, and hence the average cost of production is closer to marginal cost for the same amount of investment. This results in more competitive pricing and higher market share.

Companies that can respond swiftly to their customers benefit not only themselves but also their customers. Both the company and its customers can:

i. work with less inventories;
ii. make just-in-time procurement decisions resulting in fewer change orders;
iii. be more profitable because less cash is tied up in the current assets;
iv. attain their desired characteristics faster and create more value.

Thus, fast companies are more valuable because they create more value for their customers.

Managing information well is the basis for speed in competition. Processes designed for speed bring several advantages. The Japanese Kanban system had a competitive advantage even prior to the digital era because it could use information efficiently. In the digital era, sharing the information within the entire value chain and making efficient use of it requires use of technology. E-company practices increase speed.

Since speed also requires flexibility, responding to changing circumstances such as technology, market, or customer expectations is also easier for the fast company. Fast companies are more innovative, more responsive, and hence more profitable.

Speed is infectious. Suppliers, distribution channels, and customers that work with the fast company also gain speed and get into the habit of acting fast. This is evidenced by the higher value placed on time in more developed markets.

Speed facilitates unique service. It reduces transaction costs by reducing the time between information gathering and decision making, and adds to customer focus by responsiveness.

Preventing loss of time increases investment productivity and enables more production for the same or less amount of investment. Speed reduces the risk of investing in outdated technology.

MANAGEMENT IN FAMILY-OWNED COMPANIES

Of all businesses in the world, as in Turkiye, 80% are family businesses. It is not just small businesses, 40% of the top 500 businesses are family firms. Yet, 70% of all family businesses cannot be passed on to the next generation and among those that can 50% do not make it to the third generation. A typical family business has a life of 24 years.

The greatest advantage of family businesses is their ability to grow and make decisions rapidly: a shared past and value norms, mutual trust, and efficient communication enable them to move fast on their feet when it comes to taking decisions and implementing them.

As generations pass and families expand, business and family roles get mixed up, business matters intrude in family relations, the vagueness of profit distribution principles, mixing up business logic and emotions all add up to bring the end of the family business. Those families that successfully pass the business from one generation to another usually have the following common characteristics: they have a strict separation of business, partnership, and family matters and they have separate mechanisms to resolve problems in each sphere.

It helps to form a family council that allows the family to treat business matters with the seriousness and professional discipline they require. To prepare a family constitution that clearly defines the vision, the mission, and the values of the family and to plan for intrafamily communication, individual development and the transfer of power from one generation to another also help matters significantly. To work with an independent and trusted consultant makes the acceptance of these plans more palatable for all members.

The success of family businesses does not rely solely on preparing these principles and drafting up plans. Family businesses, too, must do their job well like all other competitive enterprises. To that end they must be able to manage all human resources as well as the family resources and apply modern management techniques. The potential for success thus increases, if those with actual or potential leadership qualities are trained and given a chance to accumulate valuable experience as early as possible and with as much care as possible.

A better management of family businesses in our countries and their adoption of future planning techniques may also contribute to our social welfare. Therefore, those who are in charge of family businesses should always be cognizant of the fact that their responsibility does not end with managing the present but requires that they take planning the future seriously.

THE CHARACTERISTICS OF A GOOD CEO

One of the key responsibilities of the boards in order to provide good governance to the company is to make the right choice for the CEO and reward him and his team appropriately.

The difference between a good leader and a good manager is summarized as follows: a good manager does the job right, and a good leader makes sure the job is done right. A CEO however, is expected to be both a good manager and a good leader.

A successful CEO needs to have a number of characteristics. First and foremost is the ability to set a vision for the company and to focus every resource on realizing this vision. The ability to deal with complexity and to focus corporate resources on a common vision improves the effectiveness of resource utilization.

Another key characteristic of a CEO is high ethical standards. The tone at the top determines the tune in the middle. As one of the important responsibilities is not only to create value but also to preserve value, their performance is predicated on the sustainability of the corporation. Any departure from high ethical standards seriously harms the sustainability of the organization. Furthermore, a CEO with high ethical standards improves the trustworthiness of the corporation and becomes a role model for the rest of the organization.

A good CEO has to have good communication skills and an ability to motivate people. In today's organizations, spanning a number of geographies, the ability to keep people motivated throughout the organization and focused on the vision requires good communication and persuasion skills. Any organization that is to be successful needs to mobilize not only its own resources but also of the resources of all its stakeholders. The CEO's role is critical in mobilizing those resources.

Good management requires good teamwork. Therefore, one of the key characteristics of a good CEO is his ability to select, develop, and motivate people. Having a good understanding of the strengths and weaknesses of each team member and how to motivate them is an important leadership skill. Good leadership is also being a good coach. Therefore what is important is not only forming a good team, but also developing the people in it.

A CEO has to be able to make tough decisions under conditions of uncertainty. In many instances, being indecisive or a populist will hurt the company. Therefore, a good CEO needs to have a high degree of self-confidence to face reality and take decisions with less than perfect knowledge. Having a high degree of self-confidence does not mean a claim to know everything, but rather accepting the fact that taking no decision is the worst decision.

While taking care not to be indecisive under uncertainty, CEOs need to be open to conflicting information. Adapting to changing conditions does not mean indecisiveness. A good captain has to be able to make judgments on environmental conditions and alter course if necessary to reach the destination.

Also, the ability to take precautions and manage risks is a key leadership skill. Preparing the minds of the leadership team for potential risks helps identify early signs in different risk areas and to deal with them effectively.

Creating loyalty to the company is also an important attribute of a good CEO. Companies that have the loyalty of their employees, customers, and suppliers are successful in their business results. Creating loyalty does not come about only by impartial evaluation and reward systems, but also by the actions and values of the leader of the company.

Some important principles need to be observed to create loyalty:

Consistency of word and deed – actions speak louder than words. Technological developments facilitate rapid communication, which means inconsistencies can surface rapidly as well. So in the words of the great Sufist thinker Mevlana, "appear as you are, be as you appear." When Johnson and Johnson stood behind its mission of human health as its primary concern, by withdrawing all Tylenols from the market when one box was found to be contaminated, its credibility in the market was strongly reinforced.

Make life simple – the simpler the strategy of a company can be conveyed, the easier it is to understand by the people who put it into effect, and the easier to be consistent. Even if the analyses to formulate the strategy are complicated, to make the communication of it simple is an important task of the CEO. Clarity of the organizational structure is an element that makes life simple for the customer and commends his loyalty. Setting up a limited number of easy to understand major performance criteria allows ease of measuring performance and its development. This increases the satisfaction and loyalty of the employees.

Base reward on loyalty generating behavior – a lot of companies reward short-term profitability generating performance more than long-term loyalty generating behavior. To reward managers that develop their teams rather than those that are only concerned with tasking them hard in the name of productivity increases employee loyalty. Similarly, when offering opportunities to attract new customers, the same should be offered to existing ones to positively impact customer loyalty.

Establish win–win relationships – to take care that all stakeholders in the company benefit from the relationship is an important way to promote loyalty. Unhappy employees cannot make customers happy. Unhappy suppliers cannot be expected to make investments for the company. It must be remembered that every company is part of a value chain, and that the chain is only as strong as its weakest link. Relationships based on a win–win principle make the chain stronger and increase its competitiveness.

Make the right choices – creating a system that generates loyalty requires that all the links are guided by the same principles. Selecting employees, suppliers, and customers that adhere to the same values enhances loyalty. Company culture and systems can be organized to support long-term profitable relationships.

Listen and speak openly – it is important to encourage open dialogue supported by data with all the stakeholders. Furthermore, the messages should be conveyed clearly and consistently to increase trust and loyalty in relationships.

DEVELOPING FUTURE LEADERS

An important factor in sustainability of an institution is the ability to develop new leaders. Whether it is a family-owned company, a publicly-traded company, armed forces, or an academic institution, the success rate of those that cannot develop people with leadership qualities at all levels is much less than those that retain the capability. Institutions that put an emphasis on developing leadership skills have sustainable success.

Leadership is the ability to activate people towards a common goal. On average, each person changes the actions of 250 people in one form or another. In this sense, everyone is a leader. However, what differentiates leaders is the number of people influenced, the impact and sustainability of the change, and the size of resources mobilized for the common goal.

A leader, at any level, has the ability to motivate a group toward a common goal, gain their confidence, and provide the discipline and conviction to overcome any difficulties to reach that goal.

In any institution, there is a need for good managers as well as good leaders. Good managers make healthy plans and budgets, choose the right people for the job and manage their performance, and control efficient use of resources. Generally, people that are successful in the core operations of the institutions assume management positions. They tend to manage internal resources over which they have direct control.

However, leadership requires managing external resources as well. To develop a good leader requires extensive exposure to important aspects of the areas critical to the institution. However, if performance criteria are determined only as the ability to fulfill assigned responsibilities, then situation specific capabilities are developed in favor of certain other leadership qualities.

This is why institutions that emphasize leader development evaluate the people they have identified on a broader scale beyond their assigned responsibilities. Capabilities beyond generating new ideas, such as getting support for these ideas within or outside the institution, influencing not only the group under his responsibility but other parts of his relationship network, imposing stretching goals and generating enthusiasm for those goals through concise communication, gathering people behind a goal, and developing the team, all come under evaluation. These are leadership qualities that are fluid between positions and institutions.

Motivating potential leaders, creating opportunities to test these capabilities, and providing regular feedback is the task of existing leaders. In summary, an important characteristic of corporate leadership is focusing on developing leaders from within the organization. This approach gives more confidence in the future of the institution.

HUMAN RESOURCES MANAGEMENT

Human resources management is not just the most important job of a specialized department in the company but rather of management starting at the top. The human resources department is a support function to management.

To manage human resources well there must first be an organization structure that fits the strategy. Good managers realize the structural changes as strategy and conditions warrant such change. The organization structure of a design company is different from that of a textile manufacturer.

An organization is as good as the quality of the people that form it. Therefore attracting quality human resources is an important task. Human resource management must include attracting resources from outside the company as well as managing those that are part of the company. Utilizing resources in line with their particular capabilities increases their chances of success and development motivation.

Another important step in human resource management is establishing the system of pay and side benefits, administering the system fairly, and keeping the system up to date with market developments and priorities of the institution. Having a good human resource management system is necessary to maintain consistency in this regard.

Human resources management systems are like parts of machinery that work together. Capabilities are at the basis of the relationship of the parts. Identifying, measuring, and developing these capabilities of both existing and potential employees is an important human resource function.

Managing and developing the performance of employees is at the core of human resource management. Measuring performance, establishing the incentive and motivation systems, and training and career planning are integral parts of this function. Just as in every other issue, not just systems, but management approach determines the success of this function.

The cornerstones of this approach are the realistic determination of performance targets, sharing the company objectives openly and regularly with employees, promoting success stories and their rewards as examples, and providing opportunities for staff development.

The coaching of good performers and training by experienced managers, and involving other levels and parts of the organization in the evaluation help institutionalize the human resource management.

Managing human resources requires having a good grasp of the whole of the business, strategies, and the factors that contribute to profitability, good communication skills to motivate and guide people, common sense, and a sound sense of fairness.

Managing people in the information age requires a depth of knowledge. A tough competitive environment, high degree of mobility, and high developmental motivation necessitates sound human resource and diversity management for success.

Structuring the Organization

Companies are set up to achieve specific purposes, and mobilize resources toward that purpose. Structuring the human resource element in line with the purpose of the company is a determining factor in the effectiveness of the institution.

The major problem in organizations is the fact that structures are not focused on realizing the purpose. The organization structure of an institution is not an end in itself but a vehicle. Designing this vehicle well is one of the priority steps to achieve the objectives of the institution. When strategies or conditions change, the organization structure must inevitably change.

For this reason, in structuring or restructuring an organization, strategic objectives must be given careful consideration. Objectives must be clearly defined prior to the structuring.

An important consideration in the restructuring process is an evaluation of the existing staff capabilities on the basis of the requirements of the strategy. An organization designed without a proper understanding of the qualifications and capabilities of the existing human resource base cannot achieve the desired results.

Another subject that merits careful consideration prior to organizational structuring is the evaluation of the institution's financial, technological, and infrastructural resources.

In designing the organization structure, the main processes to reach strategic objectives must be identified, and facilitating coordination to manage these processes must be part of the design.

That every level and position adds value contributes to the effectiveness of the organization. Therefore, another guiding principle in designing the structure is that it should be as simple as possible. Determining what functions to keep within the organization and which to outsource is an important input into the planning.

Another area to address is the definition of responsibilities, powers, and key performance indicators for each unit in the organization. If each unit in the organization is equipped with the authority to meet its responsibilities, and is held accountable, management of the organization becomes simpler. Organizational structure and titles should be clear enough to all stakeholders. Also, areas of expertise should be given the latitude to develop their area.

In order that the organization structure can be flexible to adapt to changing circumstances, dimensions that allow for flexibility should be determined.

Organization structuring efforts should take into account all stakeholders in the governance system. Otherwise, sustainability and implementability of the effort will be questionable.

The effort should also take the opportunity to identify the necessary changes in the infrastructure. In particular, information flow and incentive and reward systems should be consistent with company objectives. Successful achievement of strategic objectives necessitates successful design of organizational structure.

Successful Teams

Success of teams set up either on a temporary or permanent basis also impact the level of creativity and the transformation and development of institutions. Setting up successful teams is an important corporate requirement.

In the information age, institutions need to benefit from the brain power of all employees. Without proper motivation, ownership, and participation, it is difficult to take advantage of people's brain power.

Successful institutions become organized in teams rather than in hierarchical structures.

Organizing a team for success requires their upfront agreement on a common goal. The goal should be hard enough to make a difference, yet realistic enough for the team members to be motivated to reach it. Sufficient time needs to be invested in communication at the outset to reach the agreement. Including the team members in the stage of formulating and clarifying the goal creates ownership of the goal.

Establishing milestones in reaching the goal and their monitoring by the team is a requisite for team building. A celebration at reaching milestones is a motivating factor.

Resource allocation and planning should be put into the training of the team. Training planning has two distinct objectives: enhancing or endowing capabilities to achieve the goal and developing team-working capabilities. The first differs for each team depending on their objective, but for the second, communication and problem-solving technique training is useful in developing all teams.

The authority of teams should increase as team performance increases. This serves to increase the confidence and creativity of the team. However, teams should always be cognizant of their interdependence on other teams. Even teams that manage themselves are bound by institutional targets.

Corporate incentive systems should be structured to reward team performance. Remuneration should be team based. To enable people to take different parts in different teams, capability development should be rewarded. Assignment of individuals to various teams with different roles is an effective way of developing their capabilities and maturity. Systems should be in place to enable all team members real or virtual to share information. Communication is a critical means to promote team spirit.

Corporate culture should also support teamwork and transparent communication. The self-discipline of each team member to contribute to the team's success should be monitored and encouraged. Continued success of teams requires planned change. Changing responsibilities within the team, or occasionally adding new members to the team increases the performance. Maintaining enthusiasm is an important motivational tool.

Today in particular, performance of teams determines the performance of institutions. Building successful teams is possible through a well-planned approach and application.

In-House Training

As more and more companies realize the importance of developing their human resources, they increase their training budgets. They take advantage of various training programs available in the market. Some companies even share per person training hours with the market as part of their corporate image building. Investment in training requires planning and evaluation just as capital investment plans. If human resource is our most valuable resource, then its utilization in the most efficient and productive way should be a priority for the company.

There are two major objectives of training planning: to enable the person to fulfill job requirements at company standards, and to increase the knowledge base and vision of those with high potential and prepare them for other assignments within the company.

A common mistake in planning training is measuring only the inputs. Management evaluates per person training hours, which results in related decisions being made only with regard to increasing or reducing these hours. Difficult as it is, criteria should be developed to evaluate the benefits. It will then be possible to evaluate not only "how much training," but "which training," and "from whom."

The benefits of training are best realized by making use of the training on the job. Therefore, companies should take care to create the work environment to make use of the training, or time the training to enable this. Similar to production, training is also more productive if it is "just-in-time."

Training planning should not be seen only as part of the job description of the human resources department, but as part of a people management and career planning process, which are among the most important duties of top management. Therefore, training planning should be construed by top management as an investment into the performance management and career planning process. To achieve maximum productivity from investment into human resource, the process should be managed well.

Valuing the Individual: Motivation and Participation

TQM is a management philosophy that has human fulfillment at its core. An EFQM Business Excellence Model (BEM) has been developed to measure the application effectiveness of TQM within an organization. One of the fundamental concepts of BEM is that people with a high level of motivation and participation increase the level of performance.

Another important concept in BEM is that performance that cannot be measured cannot be improved. Measuring employee motivation and participation can be realized in two ways: through perception measures, and with performance indicators.

As TQM applications among institutions increase, use of employee satisfaction surveys also increases. These surveys serve four main purposes: (1) to provide an orderly means of communication between employee and management, (2) to serve as a tool for improvement by determining impact of management actions on employees, (3) to serve as a developmental tool for employees by giving them an opportunity to make an overall assessment of issues important to the institution and to derive lessons from it, and (4) serve as a tool for early recognition of problems within the institution.

These are all important to achieve management quality. Conducting employee satisfaction surveys on a regular basis and evaluating how they change over time improves the atmosphere of trust, and accelerates continuous improvement and early problem recognition. In summary, valuing the individual brings value to the company.

Innovation and Creativity

Companies realize high value creation by developing their corporate creativity. There needs to be a right environment to foster corporate creativity. Putting together teams that have diverse experience and viewpoints increases creativity. Therefore, diversity should be used for advantage in employee selection, assignment distribution, career planning, and team formation.

In positions that particularly require creativity, to equip the employee with diverse experiences also enhances creativity. Nokia's sending teams for a few months to Little Venice in California to observe and live cutting edge new trends serves as an example.

Lifting any corporate obstacles is necessary to manage creativity. Bureaucracy, punitive action, or contempt are obstacles. A good example of strong conviction and learning from mistakes is that of Edison, who made numerous unsuccessful attempts before finally coming up with the light bulb.

Another obstacle is habit. To overcome this obstacle, various aspects of the business should be re-evaluated every so often and their suitability to changing conditions should be reassessed.

Open-mindedness enhances creativity. Companies with systems in place to make young employees, new hires from different sectors, or special customer requests heard find it easier to generate new and innovative ideas.

For an idea to become creative, it should be accepted and put into application. So marketing the idea becomes as important as generating the idea. Successful companies allocate resources to market new ideas. For instance, some distribute the product for free prior to advertising a launch to provide an opportunity to test the product.

Creativity and innovation are at the heart of business development. Small improvements are an indispensable part of the business, yet these serve to improve productivity rather than generate new businesses.

Generating a new business requires a progressive approach that carries risk. In the early stages performance may be inferior to existing businesses that have had the benefit of continuous improvement.

Continuous improvement increases the foothold of large existing players. Players like Intel are establishing themselves more firmly with increased speed of their computers. On the other hand, progressive approaches lay the groundwork for new players to take up market share. Apple taking such an approach in the 1980s and introducing the personal computer made life difficult for IBM.

Taking on the risk of turning out new technologies is a major business development effort. These new technologies are at first adopted by customers that are nonessential to existing players, and hence are not seen as initially threatening. When Sony first introduced transistor radios to the market in the 1950s, due to its cheap price, it carved out a market among students who perceived it as an opportunity to listen to their own music even though the sound quality was poor. If it was positioned to appeal to the existing set of radio listeners, its rate of success would have been much less.

A similar approach was adopted by Honda and Toyota when first entering the US market. They introduced small and cheap cars, which were not taken seriously by the existing car manufacturers.

Two points are instrumental in the success of introducing new technologies: (1) targeting customer segments that are not threatening for the existing players, and (2) targeting customer segments that cannot afford the old technology and will be able to tolerate the hiccups of the developmental stage.

Investigating thoroughly which customer needs are served increases the success rate of a new technology. Assuming that digital cameras are preferred due to the ease of editing photos leads to an emphasis of this characteristic in both marketing and product development. However, customer surveys show that digital photography is preferred because of the ability to share photos on the Internet.

Focusing on enabling the customer to do what they want rather than imposing a new behavior as a result of the new technology also increases the probability of success. It would be dangerous to defer new technology for fear it will adversely impact the existing business. This is a mistake that large players in the market tend to make because they believe they have control of the market, have image concerns, and they do not properly evaluate the opportunity cost of allowing new entrants into the market. Companies that have the courage to bring to market products that leave their existing technology behind achieve sustainable success. Hewlett Packard is one company that has not refrained from introducing new printer technologies that knocked their profitable product lines. This approach has served to establish the company image as creative and innovative, increasing its brand value.

Sony has a similar approach in introducing new products fast and receiving customer feedback about satisfaction and product performance. It must be remembered that companies that delay in embracing new technologies for fear of hurting existing profitability will lose business to others.

New technology can also be used to reach customers through new channels. Internet marketing of tickets to any cultural activity through Biletix has created value both for event organizers and for viewers.

Creativity and innovation are at the heart of growth and profitability, and can be applied at any part of the value chain.

Mistakes are Valuable Learning Opportunities

"First, get the cow out of the ditch. Second, find out how the cow got into the ditch. Third, make sure you do whatever it takes so the cow doesn't go into the ditch again" (*The Economist*, February 13, 2010). These are words of Anne Mulcahy, the former boss of Xerox, describing her approach as she (successfully) fought to revive the company.

To hide mistakes or to try to blame others are common human instincts. However, mistakes can be a golden learning opportunity, and to hide a mistake or to be afraid of admitting to one can be a missed learning opportunity.

Unsuccessful venture capital instances have hampered the development of this type of capital in developing markets. Yet it is difficult to generate value creation without taking risks or making mistakes. In countries where venture capital companies have developed, even if some ventures are unsuccessful, the experience contributes to the success of others.

In a competitive environment, success includes information and learning. The most efficient way of learning is through experience and mistakes. Not making mistakes limits learning potential. "Small" mistakes that involve testing and bearing their costs is necessary. Not allocating resources for such mistakes is the "big mistake."

To encourage creativity, organizations should:

1. provide an environment for testing ideas and allocate resources for experiments;

2. encourage admitting to mistakes as soon as possible. Some companies even reward sharing mistakes;
3. make detailed analyses of mistakes and determine their root causes;
4. invest into systems to prevent mistakes from recurring;

Leaders should assume the important role of promoting constructive criticism rather than blame for mistakes. Leaders should eradicate fear of failure in learning and development to accelerate creativity. The prevailing atmosphere should be one of "taking calculated risks" rather than "not doing anything for fear of failure." A transparent environment that encourages learning from mistakes also improves trust.

Yamaha's Piano

An example which illustrates the importance of creativity and innovation in success is that of the piano. The piano is a durable musical instrument that has not fundamentally changed since the time of Mozart. Many students of the piano never get good enough to move to a better version. Therefore, this expensive instrument is not renewed for a few generations, some of them becoming purely decorative. It is estimated that there are 40 million such pianos.

After reaching a 40% market share with a lot of struggle, Yamaha observed that the market had actually shrunk by 10% annually. Yamaha also noted Koreans coming into the market with cheaper models. In view of the shrinking market size, the options were to respond by reducing prices, investing to improve quality, or getting out of the business. None of the options was attractive for Yamaha. In response, Yamaha studied the product and its customers in detail, and devised an alternative strategy to the unattractive options.

The results of the studies were not promising. A lot of the 40 million pianos were not being played at all. Moreover, since playing the piano required a lot of determination, those who did not show the required discipline regretted owning pianos.

This meant that the market was saturated even for quality products. According to the famous Japanese strategist Kenichi Ohmae, Yamaha was successful under such difficult circumstances by taking a creative approach after careful investigation of its market.

Creating value was not going to come through new piano manufacture, but rather through a different use of the existing ones. All the unused pianos could be put to use to listen to world famous pianists at home! Yamaha developed a technology that had the ability to hit the piano keys in 92 different kinds of speed and strength. This digitally based technology could perfectly replicate notes onto computer disks. People that had the new Yamaha product installed into their pianos could listen to the concert recordings or CDs of famous pianists as if live from their pianos at home.

With the introduction of this new technology, people that wanted to have "concerts" at home, people that played other musical instruments but wanted piano accompaniment, people that wanted to record their own to be played at their friends' pianos all showed great interest in the new product.

In a market that had been shrinking by 10% for five years in a row, there was suddenly a marketing opportunity for a US$2500 product for 40 million pianos. This novelty approach expanded the piano market in different ways. Those that wanted to listen to famous pianists like Fazıl Say play at their home started maintaining and tuning their pianos. Worldwide piano maintenance market hit a US$1.6 billion turnover, showing an increase in maintenance as well as new product sales.

This development revived people's desire to play the piano, and the number of people that started lessons and sales of training videos boomed. Approaching the market with a customer point of view brought Yamaha success. The piano became more than an instrument to play, it became a source of entertainment on which you could listen to music as well. Given the big investment of time to learn to play the piano, the relatively small investment to enjoy it was attractive to customers. This created a new market for millions of idle pianos all around the world thanks to Yamaha's brilliant approach.

This led to a new market being created for digital instruments. Today the market for digital pianos is much larger than that for classical pianos. Digital instruments have variety of use and are more attractively priced.

Yamaha was able to understand that a piano investment was not just an investment into a musical instrument, but rather a time investment as well. Therefore, Yamaha added value by providing a reduced emphasis on time allocation and more ways to enjoy the investment. Once again, looking at the investment through customers' eyes ended in success.

TRUST WITHIN THE CORPORATION

Hard to replicate assets are critical in competition. Corporate culture is one such asset in achieving a sustainable competitive advantage. While trustworthiness and reputation are discerning competitive characteristics for the institution, these should not only be taken into account in relationships with outside parties. An atmosphere of trust within the institution among employees is also a determinant in company performance.

Three different dimensions should be taken into account in establishing an atmosphere of trust:

 i. trust in clarity and transparency of communication, that impacts information sharing and problem solving;
 ii. trust in personalities and their honesty and loyalty, that impacts adherence to written or verbal agreements;
 iii. trust in capabilities that impact the belief and behavior of individuals in achieving company goals.

Trust in communication allows ease of information sharing, open and constructive criticism, correcting mistakes by admitting to them, and protecting confidential information from third parties.

Trust in personalities allows corporations to realize consistent strategies, to enhance corporate values, to stick to commitments, and to develop win–win relationships. This trust element, which is the basis of consistent corporate behavior, serves to increase the brand value of corporations.

To establish trust in capabilities within the corporation, clear recognition of delegated authority, participation of employees in decision making, teamwork with different groups, and training and development programs are necessary.

Managers have to have the self-confidence to delegate responsibility to foster trust. The most effective way to inspire trust is not through verbal communication but through behavioral communication.

Sometimes the most trusted will betray the trust. Therefore, corporations must not neglect the installation of an adequate control and audit system. While lessons must be learned from instances of betrayed trust this must not stand in the way of the creation of an atmosphere of trust.

SHARING INFORMATION

The most important input into value creation is information. This is the "information age" because the most important investments are not into physical assets but into information. The fact that Microsoft is one of the most valuable companies in the world attests to this fact.

One of the main differentiating factors of information is that it increases when it is shared. Therefore, the most effective way of increasing and developing information is sharing it.

Developments in communication technologies in particular, the emphasis on transparency, and the availability of information generated by public funds all point to a new era. Structuring organizations to maximize information sharing are more successful in this era. When Microsoft is way ahead of its large competitors, a company like Linux can pose a threat with its free information sharing model.

For information to increase as it is shared, it needs to be shared between parties with parity with respect to the information. Therefore, information should be shared with similarly informed outside parties as well as within the organization. Information sharing structures formed by people with similar levels of knowledge even if they work at different institutions are called "expertise guilds."

These structures tie membership with personal choices. Continued membership depends on motivation and input of members. If the level of knowledge starts deepening within the structure, it is dissolved in favor of new structures.

These e-guilds can be set up between different geographies of the same large company, or between different companies, with no time or location restrictions. They create a medium to share best practice examples and speed up development in the entire system. Coming together with other people of expertise in the same profession also provides for an opportunity for self-evaluation and hence, development.

Job satisfaction is higher for professionals working in companies that encourage these guilds. This increases loyalty to the company, as well as attracting qualified professionals.

The expertise guilds build up the capacity of companies and individuals for problem solving. Professionals that become familiar with problems in different environments accumulate knowledge and capability. People with diverse experiences working on the same problem increase the capacity for solving it.

Companies that support the guilds also gain new business ideas or fields. The aim of the World Bank to eventually turn itself into an "information bank" provides a good example of an effort to institutionalize expertise guilds.

Expertise guilds are yet another tool for good human resource management for value creation. Companies that support them will develop faster in the information age.

SOCIAL RESPONSIBILITY

When investing, should the only criterion be how much return will be achieved? How do we feel if we have invested in the lucrative shares of a mining company whose workers in their African mines are losing their lives because of the working conditions?

The social responsibility concept is playing a bigger and bigger role in global investment decisions:

"Marketing people say consumers are increasingly trying to do good as they spend. Research in 2008 by Cone, a brand consultancy, found that 79% of consumers would switch to a brand associated with a good cause, up from 66% in 1993, and that 38% have bought a product associated with a cause, compared with 20% in 1993." … [This is saying that if firms cannot] "make products that can be marketed as ethical in their own right, such as 'fair trade' goods, they are increasingly trying to take an ordinary product and boost its moral credentials with what one marketing guru calls 'embedded generosity.'" (*The Economist*, February 13, 2010)

This becomes evident in three different dimensions:

1. The industry in which the company is operating – people think twice about investing in human life threatening industries such as arms or tobacco. They are also more cognizant of the value added to society beyond the value created for the company.
2. Adherence to corporate governance principles – whether a company has a culture of consistency, responsibility, accountability, fairness, transparency, and effectiveness deployed throughout the organization is critical not only to its success but to how investors evaluate the company. The quality of a company management is as determined by the quality of the corporate structure as it is by the quality of its managers. The corporate structure should inspire trust in all its stakeholders and in financial markets.
3. Contribution to society – the extent to which a company allocates resources to solving issues has an impact on how investors view the company. Successful companies differentiate themselves not only by their products or services but also by their contribution to society. Societal respect increases the value of a company. Studies show that taking social responsibility into account in investments also impacts returns positively. Companies with social responsibility are highly valued by their stakeholders and hence carry less risk.

CORPORATE CITIZENSHIP

Companies have four basic social responsibilities:

1. **economical** – to be productive and profitable;
2. **legal** – to observe the law;
3. **ethical** – to behave in accordance with ethical norms and expectations;
4. **social** – to volunteer to contribute to solving social issues.

International organizations such as the UN, EU, OECD, and World Bank all place emphasis on social responsibility. For sustainable economic development, the private sector has to increase their interest and support of the society of which they are a part.

Successful companies understand that earning public trust increases the value of their company. They also understand that an inclination to turn their social contributions to the benefit of the company constitutes an insincerity that is more harmful than beneficial.

Sincere efforts on the other hand do benefit the company. Their social contributions increase the mind share in society, thereby increasing the value of their brand. In an age where information is so readily available, such contributions increase the depth, intensity, and quality of the relationship of the company with its customers.

Social contribution also attracts well-rounded qualified people to the company, and earns their loyalty. People feel closer to institutions that take an interest in and assume responsibility for issues of the society. Companies that emphasize value creation for their society also inspire higher work motivation for their employees.

A lot of international funds are taking company social responsibility activities into their evaluation prior to making an investment into a company. Companies that emphasize social contribution can access more international funds based on the London FT4GOOD index. Companies with high levels of social contributions are also highly regarded by public administrations as well.

Cooperation with reputable civil society institutions increases the effectiveness of the company's social contribution. When resources and management expertise of a company are combined with the experience of a civil society institution, it increases the quality of the solutions. Just as in business life, focus and effective cooperation produce efficient results. Efficient results add to society, as well as to the company.

Currently, the majority of the world's population is living in countries run by democratic systems (albeit to a varying degree) and have market based economies. Economic, technological, and political developments increase interdependence. Improving the welfare of the society in a sustainable way requires companies as well as individuals to take responsibility.

Companies understand that global citizenship brings global responsibilities as well as rights. CEOs that are in charge of substantial resources are expected to have global leadership capabilities. At a World Economic Forum meeting, CEOs of 40 leading multinational companies, among them ABB, Coca Cola, Deutsche Bank, McDonald's, Merck, Siemens, and UBS, signed a "Global Citizenship" declaration. In addition to these well known names, the list includes companies from Chile, South Africa, and Saudi Arabia.

Corporate citizenship is defined covering three main ideologies:

1. That the company will respect human rights, institute healthy and safe working conditions, protect the environment, and avoid any corruption in its operations anywhere in the world.
2. That company activities definition extends to include its market, suppliers, civil society institutions, and public sector relationships, and that it has to be in close cooperation with all these stakeholders.
3. That the above are embraced by the company Chairman, Board of Directors, CEO, and management teams as responsibilities.

Top management of companies aware of their corporate citizenship responsibilities are expected to lead on this issue, to define the concept, to identify company stakeholders clearly, to pursue a result oriented strategy in this respect, and to be accountable for results. Top management leading on the issue is demonstrated by their clear communication of the company's aims, principles, and values with respect to their social responsibility both within and without the company, and their commitment by their actions.

Company leaders are expected to articulate the corporate citizenship concept and why it is necessary in investor relations, general assembly meetings, annual reports, and various other platforms within and outside the company. They are also expected to devote time to civil society institutions and other similar platforms to make the world a better place to live.

Corporate citizenship concept is defined differently for different companies. What a pharmaceutical company can do for society is different from what a cement company can do. Where they operate, and the cross-sections of society that they impact will also be different, thus determining who to target and with what aim is important in pursuing results.

Social responsibility should be taken seriously. Planning and management of this subject should also be part of board meeting agendas on a regular basis. Performance criteria should be identified and performance monitored. Cooperation with civil society institutions and other similar organizations should be developed. Creative solutions and future leaders that take initiative in the process should be encouraged.

Accountability is critical to earning respect as a global citizen. This is why it is important to determine which activity will be measured and how, and to regularly gauge performance against the criteria, and share the results. Modest and realistic measures at the outset can be stretched over time for more ambitious targets. Even when targets are not reached, transparency must be maintained. All of the foregoing serves to increase societal trust. Companies that lead in the global citizenship concept raise their profiles beyond their own borders, and also contribute to the esteem of their countries.

RESPECT

We started out this section on good governance with preparing for the future on the company dimension with an emphasis on trust. This entire section on the importance of building trust points to the ultimate purpose of earning and keeping respect.

We can therefore conclude and summarize this section on the basis of respect. People or companies that command respect in society get a chance to mobilize more resources. Respect is hard earned over a long period of time through consistent behavior, but is easy to lose overnight. Consistency in word and deed, and active communication of the reasons for deed form the foundation of earning respect.

As companies earn respect, they raise the value of their brands, and therefore the value of their companies. This is why they take special care to protect their reputation. Earning respect requires consistency on many dimensions. First, they must create value by differentiating their product or service. Growing and competing successfully to generate profits is an important step.

Companies are evaluated not only according to their financial results but also according to their adherence to good governance principles of Consistency, Responsibility, Accountability, Fairness, Transparency, and Effectiveness Deployed throughout the organization (CRAFTED).

Consistency of values, communications, and actions is key to earning respect. Responsibility toward the resources entrusted to the company, to demonstrate high standards of performance, adherence to legal requirements, and ethical behavior, to mobilize resources to contribute to resolution of social issues, also earns respect for the company. Accountability in timeliness and integrity of disclosures to all stakeholders and fairness in their treatment are integral to earning trust and therefore respect.

Transparency of decisions and information sharing enhances respectability. Effectiveness of governance by separation of powers of implementation and control and monitoring is also an important contributor to the respect that the company commands. The example of Johnson and Johnson previously discussed demonstrates how trust can be developed from a potential disaster. An example of the reverse that shows how trust can be eroded comes from the actions of the bottled water company Perrier 20 years ago. Their fizzy water was found to be contaminated with benzene. The company recalled all its bottles, but its explanation for what had gone wrong kept changing. Two years later, weakened, it succumbed to a hostile bid from Nestle, but neither its sales, nor its brand, which once stood for purity, ever fully recovered.

Companies are constantly showing efforts to increase their products and services but also customer satisfaction. To earn respect, a company should emphasize effective communication of not only its products and services but of its corporate values.

NOTES

1   See http://www.economist.com/node/15498249.
2   Argüden, Yılmaz, *Boardroom Secrets: Corporate Governance for Quality of Life*, Palgrave Macmillan, 2009.
3   BRIC, or the BRICs, is Goldman Sachs investment bank's 2003 designation of Brazil, Russia, India, and China (BRIC) as potentially the four most dominant economies by the year 2050.
4   Next Eleven, or N-11, are the countries – Bangladesh, Egypt, Indonesia, Iran, Mexico, Nigeria, Pakistan, the Philippines, South Korea, Turkiye, and Vietnam – identified by Goldman Sachs investment bank as having a high potential of becoming the world's largest economies in the twenty-first century, along with the BRICs.
5   Such as experience in management of mega projects or local consumer trends.
6   The author is a board member of Anadolu Efes, Coca Cola İcecek, and Vestel.
7   Koc Holding, which controls Tupras and other companies (such as Arcelik, Tofas, Otokar, and Yapı Kredi Bank) with governance ratings between 8.00 and 8.25, has three international members on its board.
8   Ulker has international members in its Godiva subsidiary.
9   See Argüden, Yılmaz, *Boardroom Secrets: Corporate Governance for Quality of Life*, Palgrave Macmillan, 2009, Chapter 1, for a description of such common attributes and behaviors for board members.
10 The author was a member of the Board of Directors for Borusan Telecom.

11 United Nations Global Compact is a strategic policy initiative to encourage institutions to align their operations with the universally accepted principles of human rights, labor rights, environment, and anticorruption. By facilitating transparency, dialogue, and the dissemination of best practices, the Global Compact effectively encourages the implementation of good corporate citizenship and sustainability.

12 The author thanks the Women in Business unit of IFC, Brodie Jessica Mcnabb, for the data and information provided for this section.

13 Joy, Lois, Carter, Nancy, Wagner, Harvey M., and Narayanan, Sriram "The Bottom Line: Corporate Performance and Women's Representation on Boards," *Catalyst*, 2007, available from: http://www.catalyst.org/file/139/bottom%20line%202.pdf.

14 McKinsey & Company, Inc., *Women Matter: Gender Diversity, A Corporate Performance Driver*, 2007.

15 McKinsey & Company, Inc., *Women Matter: Gender Diversity, A Corporate Performance Driver*, 2007.

16 Brown, David A.H., Brown, Debra L., and Anastasopoulos, Vanessa., *Women on Boards: Not Just the Right Thing...But the "Bright" Thing*, The Conference Board of Canada, May 2002, available from: http://www.europeanpwn.net/files/women_on_boards_canada.pdf.

17 New Zealand Ministry of Women's Affairs, *Women on Boards: Why women on boards are good for business*, May 2009, available from: http://www.mwa.govt.nz/women-on-boards/women-on-boards-why-women-on-company-boards-are-good-for-business-1.

CHAPTER 7

Good Governance Starts with the Individual

We are creatures of our habits.

'God helps those who help themselves.' (Benjamin Franklin).

The basic element of any institution, and therefore any governance mechanism, is the individual, the citizen. Good governance is much more than processes, rights, and responsibilities and involves elements of culture and a climate to promote the right kinds of behavior. Therefore, in order to improve the quality of governance in all our institutions, we need start with the individual.

Hence, the individual wishing to contribute to improving the quality of life by shaping the future must start with himself. He has to make an example of himself, and plant the seeds to shaping his environment by sharing and disseminating his own vision of the future. Such an individual understands that his own actions ultimately have an impact on sustainable development and world peace, that he must attain the wisdom to shed egoism and to prioritize creating value for mankind, and that he must assume a responsibility for the future.

Preparing for the future and continuously improving quality of life is a philosophy of life that can be adopted both at the individual and society level. The individual is the cornerstone of life. There is a two-dimensional process for the individual: on the one hand, he must develop his patterns of behavior to prepare for his own future and improve his own quality of life. On the other hand, other segments of society should provide for an environment that is conducive to such an effort by the individual. This interaction will pave the way for a natural evolution of societal values.

The aim of the individual is to attain personal happiness, and to strive to improve his quality of life both materially and spiritually. Achieving this is within the realm of possibility for the individual prepared for the future. But first and foremost, he must understand that in order not to drift about like a dry leaf, life and time can, and must be, managed.

POWER OF POSITIVE THINKING

The first step in this direction is to think positively and approach life positively. Everyone wishing to improve his quality of life should learn to think positively. Thoughts impact on beliefs, beliefs impact on attitudes, and attitudes impact on how we interact with our environment. An individual with a healthy mind has a healthy body as well, thereby already improving his quality and longevity of life with his positive thinking.

In developing positive thinking abilities, it is an effective first step to benefit from the experience of others. If we identify people around us with such abilities, we can start by taking them as role models to develop our own positive thinking.

A prerequisite to developing this ability is for the individual to be at peace with himself. Consistency in thought, discourse, and deed is essential to such an inner peace, and if there is disparity between them, it will be damaging both to the trust placed in the person by others and to his inner tranquility.

Sometimes an individual is his own worst critic. Rather than dwell on one's mistakes, it is more constructive to learn from them. Positive thinking is not denying our mistakes or ignoring our shortcomings, but seeing them as an opportunity for improvement, making plans and taking action to prevent mistakes from happening again.

This will also enable a more positive interaction with people around us. If we were to consider for a moment the difficulties of being stranded on an island, we can appreciate the importance of interaction with the environment in our lives. Improving the quality of this interaction will improve the quality of our life.

To be able to think positively, we must try to scratch negative words from our vocabulary. This will help develop the ability to see the positive side to every occasion, because words impact on our thoughts and our perception.

An important input to positive living is to take responsibility in our approach to life, while maintaining a degree of flexibility. We must understand that what we want to achieve in life will not happen by itself, and that we must show the effort to make it happen. We must also understand that making the effort to shape our future does not mean we can determine it.

Therefore, learning to accept the realities is important to our mental health. However, accepting realities does not mean we have to submit to them. What is important is to identify what parts of reality we can change and to act on it constructively.

To think and live positively, an individual must have confidence in himself and in others around him. Life can be improved by those who feel they can change it. Those determined people with firm beliefs and with confidence in themselves and the people around them improve not only the quality of their own lives, but also of those around them, becoming a source of contentment.

There are two big forces in life: fear and belief. To be able to think positively, one must conquer one's fears. The most effective vehicle to conquer fears is belief. Doing your best to change things in your favor and then believing that they will turn out for the best will relieve stress and enable a healthier life. Regular physical and mental exercise will also develop positive thinking and lead to a healthy and balanced life.

Life is not a collection of ends but a process of means to get them. To make a conscious effort in the process of reaching our goal, to be consistent, and to inspire confidence in people around us are sources of contentment far bigger than the end we achieve.

An important lasting result of this process is the learning we acquire. Continuously striving to learn is the cornerstone of development. This effort also contributes to our ability to accept reality and to discern what we can change.

The people who believe in what they do have a lot of enthusiasm toward it. This enthusiasm leads them to succeed and to make positive impact. This is why it is important for people to try to do things in their life that they enjoy.

The resource that is most equitably distributed in life is time. Everyone has a 24 hour day. Using time effectively and being bold and far sighted enough to take the necessary steps to shape your future also contributes to positive thinking.

Positive thinking also has affection at its core. To be able to think positively, you have to like people, and be excited at the thought of making a difference for them. To help others with heartfelt effort is the key to feeling good. There are two values that grow when shared: affection and knowledge. The person who shares his affection and knowledge has an enriched life.

SUCCESSFUL PEOPLE ARE THOSE WHO CAN MANAGE LIFE

Successful people think positively and use the force of thinking positively. They have goals, motivation, and self discipline. They instigate positive and important changes not only in their own but also others' lives as well. Research shows that successful people have a lot of traits in common. Above all else, they have self-confidence and believe in their own worth. This gives them the courage and enthusiasm to be innovative. They are not afraid to reach high. By reaching and focusing high, they take the biggest step to getting there.

Successful people have personal goals and values in life. They have a vision of how their success will impact their world and therefore know what mission they are serving. These people have clear and realistic expectations about their personal goals, and develop and apply strategies to get there. These strategies include improving their own capabilities, and long-term planning.

Successful people also take responsibility for their actions and their future. A responsible person takes initiative, takes calculated risk, identifies steps to shape his future, and is not afraid to take these steps. He takes special care to visualize the future. The first step to realizing the life you wish for is to imagine it. Another way to realizing is to share it with others. This will enable you to make your dreams more specific and to anticipate potential issues.

Setbacks along the way are not the end of the road for successful people. On the contrary, they accept the challenge, learn from the experience, and show determination to overcome the obstacle.

Successful people:

- Are not afraid to face reality, benefit also from others' experience, and minimize their mistakes. If they stray from their target along the way, they correct their course.
- Are at peace with themselves. This reduces the level of stress in their lives. They are alert and fit in mind and body, and this facilitates their reaching their goals.
- Think long term and do not sacrifice long-term goals for short term gains. They concentrate on fewer but more important steps to reach their goals, and are not afraid to make sacrifices to get there.
- Differentiate themselves not only with their IQ but also with their EQ. Human relationships are important to them, and they can identify with people to gain a broader perspective. Establishing win–win relationships rather than self-centered relationships based on own interest is another characteristic common to successful people. They value the people they work with, share life with them, and in this way broaden their lives as well.

Preparing for the future and being successful is not a quick and easy effort. Successful people are constantly working on improving themselves. They are open to new experiences and new knowledge, and show interest in other people's experience and knowledge as well. Every mistake is a learning opportunity.

We can **learn to be successful** by reviewing our decision making process and behavior, observing and understanding our habits, and making the necessary changes. As long as we are doing this, we can start to make a difference and take firm steps in preparing for the future. All the described characteristics of successful people can be learned.

MANAGING TIME IS MANAGING LIFE

Time is very valuable, because it is life itself. Therefore, what best defines a person and his life is how he uses his time. People who want to improve their life quality must first learn to use their time well. In how we use our time, we must not only think of today, but also of tomorrow. Those who can invest in their future are awarded the opportunity to fulfill the desired outcome for their future.

Time is a limited resource that is irreversible, unstoppable, and cannot be stored. Therefore, the better use we make of this limited resource, the more we can contribute to developing ourselves and our environment.

How we perceive and value time will depend on specific circumstances. As an example, an hour with a person we enjoy being with, or two hours for a difficult exam will seem very short, but the final five minutes of a World Cup soccer game our team is leading 1–0 will seem very long. As for how valuable time can be, consider Olympic athletes who win gold medals for a split second difference. This split second means a lot to both the gold medal winner, and to the athlete who has to be content with the silver medal. On the other hand, for a person lounging in front of a television screen, an hour more or less is not very important. So we can think in terms of real or "objective" time versus perceived or "subjective" time.

In the general flow of our daily life, time passes too fast for us to consider how we perceive it, or how we value it. We may know how much money we have and how long it will last us and adjust our purchases accordingly, but we never consider doing the same with our time. However, time is more valuable to our life than money.

There is no excuse for not managing our time. This is the most democratically distributed resource. We all have 24 hours.

ALIGN USE OF TIME WITH YOUR VISION

What is important in managing time is not to prioritize the day's work, but to make sure our priorities are included in the day. People generally spend their time on tasks that require immediate handling, practically none of which contribute to their development. A lot of tasks that become urgent because we did not plan in time take up most of our daily life.

What we must really do is to determine what our goal and vision in life is then use our time to realize this vision as far as possible. In other words, we must first fill the jar with larger stones and pay attention to the larger issues, and spare the remaining time for less important tasks, and fill up the space between the large stones with pebbles and sand. Managing our time requires us to understand what our daily routines and habits are, and then determine how important these are to our life. It is critical to measure how we use our time in order that we can make the necessary changes to how we use it to reach our goals.

A person who works effectively should set aside at least 65% or 70% of his time to important tasks that are not urgent. He should use the time to plan, develop action plans to prevent possible adverse issues, delegate as much as possible, follow up on those tasks that he has already delegated, spare time to advance his social and business relationships, and develop his staff.

To be able to work effectively, the person should appoint at least one-half of a day every week to plan time and for mental exercise. In the worst case, this time can be used as spare if an urgent matter arises.

RECOMMENDATIONS FOR MANAGING OTHERS

There is one important differentiation that managers must pay attention to: their reaction to mistakes in low-priority items should be different from high-priority items. Showing the same reaction regardless of importance will reduce the desired effect for an important agenda item. If we see every mistake as an opportunity to learn, we can have a discussion with the employee about the reason and source of his mistake, enable him to understand and accept why, and lead him to make fewer mistakes going forward rather than discourage him with an excessive reaction. This will prove to be a much more effective method of dealing with employee mistakes.

When an employee comes with a problem, it should either be solved there with the employee present, or an insight or a suggestion should be provided, and the employee sent away to resolve the problem. The problem should not remain with the manager. It is best to let the employee resolve the issue whenever possible. Empowering people in this way will enable them to develop a habit of dealing with problems, motivate them, and render them more productive.

It is more productive from a time management perspective to guide others to conform to one's schedule by giving a long lead time. Since generally other participants are not used to working with long lead times, proposing meetings or study groups way ahead of time enables a manager to get other parties to agree to his own timing as well as giving him sufficient time for preparation.

We keep emphasizing the importance of identifying priorities for time management. This means we should also be in a position to turn down proposals that are not in line with our priorities. When in doubt, it helps to receive such proposals in writing and respond in writing. This helps save time that can potentially be wasted in a meeting, yet ensures that an opportunity is not overlooked. A proposal outside the interest of the individual or the company should not simply be accepted for cordial relations.

We must also be on the lookout for "time robbers." Some of the common traps are:

1. inability to identify priorities;
2. lack of planning;
3. haste;
4. procrastination;
5. unproductiveness;
6. inability to delegate;
7. indecision;
8. inability to focus;
9. inability to say no;
10. being tied to someone else's agenda.

Discipline is the most effective way of dealing with these traps. Not accepting a meeting without a predetermined agenda, meeting in a conference room rather than your office, setting a time limit at the beginning of the meeting, adhering to such a limit, and punctuality are important habits for both self-discipline and for our colleagues.

MAN IS THE CREATION OF HIS HABITS

Our habits shape our behavior. Our habits are also a way of measuring how effectively we use our time. If our purpose is to change some of our behavior to realize our life vision and make a difference, we must first understand what our habits are that shape our behavior. Self-discipline is key to success and the best way to self discipline is to make a habit of actions that are likely to support your goals. Therefore, it is useful to look at what the habits of successful people are.

A healthy life is founded on a healthy body, high level of knowledge, a relationship network based on mutual caring, and respect from and for the society we live in. All these attributes are shaped by our daily behavior.

The race is won in the training sessions before we get out on the field. Those that practice every day start off the race with a significant advantage. The soccer trainer who has kept his whole team in shape instead of his top eleven will not have anything to worry about in the long marathon of a champion's league. Those that brush their teeth every day generally have healthy teeth. Those that watch what they eat do not have to carry too much weight. Those that exercise every day have fewer injuries. Those that are in the habit of reading regularly and have the discipline to read up on their topics of interest are always current in their knowledge. Those that lose their eagerness to learn lose their chance to be up-to-date. Those that maintain sincere relationships in good days and bad accumulate a lot of goodwill and respect in their relationships. Those that do not use their time wisely cannot accumulate such social capital.

Societal trust is a fragile value that is only earned over time. Individuals that are consistent in word and deed and who look for ways of creating value for society lay the foundations for being trustworthy. In the electronic age, it is easy to catch on to falsities. Therefore, we must pay particular attention to honesty and consistency if we want to make a difference with our behavior.

Individuals have to make a habit of constantly keeping themselves informed and current with knowledge. This is a necessity particularly in business life. The more an individual meets expectations, the higher those expectations will become. A level of service that is excellent yesterday will become only sufficient today, and insufficient tomorrow. Therefore meeting expectations can only be achieved by constant development.

The level of trust and loyalty that his employer places in an individual is closely related to how intent he is to replenish his abilities and be innovative.

The quality of life of the individual is not determined only by his family and business life. The level of social responsibility we feel also is closely related to how wholesome our life is. Those who exhibit social responsibility inspire trust in people around them and receive support and loyalty in return.

Social responsibility is a prerequisite to the individual's contribution to his environment. It is not sufficient to merely take an interest in social and global issues, but to take an active part in dealing with them.

In summary, if we want to make a difference whether as an individual or as a company, we must take care to be disciplined and proactive. Large successes are built by laying a brick at a time. If any one of them is not laid right, the whole structure may collapse in time. Therefore in managing our lives or our companies, we must make a habit of stretching ourselves and making a difference.

CRITICAL DIMENSION OF LIFE: JOB AND CAREER

An individual's job has a major part in his effort to improve his quality of life. Our job not only takes up a lot of our time, but it also determines how we are defined by society. People do not generally equate work with happiness, however these two are inseparable. An individual successful in his job has gone a long way to achieving happiness.

Working is enriching in several ways. The obvious one is the material enrichment from income received. In addition to salary or wages received, health and life insurance and retirement fund contribution type benefits also serve to reduce risks and concerns about our future. So a job provides financial gains that enable the individual to manage his today, his tomorrow, and his risks.

Another enrichment element is the social environment that a job provides. Coworkers, clients, suppliers, and other relationships established at work add to the individual's quality of life and social development.

Also, a job contributes to the individual's development of his skills. A working life increases an individual's ability to deal with problems, his level of knowledge, his exposure to new technologies, and hence his overall personal development. The individual is then both successful at his current job, and better equipped for future jobs.

Finally, his working life increases the individual's sphere of influence. A job provides an individual with a number of means to be productive. Machinery and equipment, or technological means, or the supply chain, or in general the social environment at the individual's disposal are his source of power. The person with a wide sphere of influence will be sought after, and he will also be very resourceful in difficult times.

Those that cannot take advantage of all the benefits that a working life provides for them cannot be successful in building careers. Particularly, those that are not cognizant of how much of their success is due to their own merits and how much is due to the resources of the company behind them are bound to suffer when the going gets tough.

Quitting a good job makes a person choosy about the next job. If the job search continues for too long, he will not only forgo income during that period, but also the opportunities for continued development.

A working life provides a range of opportunities. It would be incorrect to assume that every working person will make the most of his job equally. To benefit from the opportunities that working life provides, one must be aware of these gains, and must show the effort to make the most of them. Those that do not establish meaningful relationships in their working life cannot benefit from the advantages that those extended relationships bring as described above and their success is inevitably limited.

People that do not plan their career on developing their capabilities lag in promotions in their jobs, and reduce their own chances for advancing through better job opportunities. Adding new capabilities complementary to existing ones makes a person more valuable throughout their careers. Therefore, a position change every 4 to 7 years is generally recommended as part of a career plan, depending on circumstances. In some professions, such as in architecture, every project constitutes a standalone experience. For these people, the content and development of projects can be considered in lieu of a position change.

Continuous development is the key to quality of life. Therefore, we can say that working is a source of contentment and not a burden. It is not an impediment to quality living, but a path to freedom.

LIVE WHILE YOU WORK; WORK WHILE YOU LIVE

Companies force people that reach their sixties to retire. Yet social security systems all over the world are in trouble as life expectancy keeps rising. Longer lives indicate that people should also work longer. People that work longer are more attached to life and hence live longer. In an era where the life expectancy of a 50-year-old already exceeds 80, working for 30 years, retiring in the fifties, and receiving pensions for 30 years, is not sustainable. If we consider that people starting working life now are likely to live into their nineties, we can imagine the looming burden of health expenditures and retirement pensions. To ease the burden on future generations, we should consider extending the retirement age.

To be able to do this, employers should be creative about employment opportunities which require reduced energy levels, yet benefit from the experience and knowledge of older people, with shorter working hours.

People over a certain age should also be receptive to taking up positions that are not as high as the positions they have held before, or consider transferring to other areas of employment. This also means as a society, we must not be judgmental about these issues, and encourage working longer. We must blend activities planned for retirement into our working life, not postpone life, and not expect that someone will take care of us as we sit back.

Raising the retirement age is a thorny issue for politicians, and they defer dealing with social security issues to future administrations.

People must be cognizant of problems regarding social security issues and plan for taking care of themselves rather than rely solely on retirement pensions.

We do not know how long we will live. However we must be prepared to live longer than the people today we think are "old," and plan our life in this way. People that live longer and healthier lives should also be productive for longer. It is important that the majority of society begins to think in this way, yet it is also important to remember to extend a helping hand to those in need as well.

CHASM IN THE MINDSET: US VERSUS THEM

Eliminating the boundaries in our mind is critical to both our own personal development as well as establishing a global society that lives in peace. To overcome the boundaries in our mind, we have to be able to have a wide horizon, control our ego, show tolerance, and clear our minds of nationalism based on discrimination. In short, we must avoid thinking in terms of "us versus them." When we establish this kind of understanding, we will have a better chance of success not only as individuals, but also as countries facilitating solutions to global issues.

Genetic mapping shows that there is in fact less than 1% difference between races. Genetic research further shows that even differences between humans and animals are not that large. It would seem that discrimination is a man-created ailment inflicting only humans. This ailment leads them to concentrate more on differences than on similarities. Many wars and struggles in history are the result of mankind pushing differences as claims to superiority.

This "us versus them" discrimination continues as a threat to global issues. There is no need to look for the reasons of such a deep chasm in differences in physical attributes, religions, or origins of geography, because the reason is the mindset. If there is a desire to think in terms of "us versus them," we start opening up the gap with others.

Imagine a country in which all the people had similar physical appearances and followed the same religion. If the children of people living in odd numbered houses were to be murdered and it was rumored that the culprits were those living in even numbered houses, rest assured that everyone walking the streets would soon start to know who was living in an odd numbered house and who was living in an even numbered house. If they were to move to different parts of the city, they would make an effort to avoid the numbers that represented "them."

All this goes to say that we must stop thinking of other people and societies in terms of "them," but start to appreciate diversity as enrichment. This change of mindset will set the stage for a peaceful future and development. The concept of "us versus them" is a means to blunt creative and innovative instincts and narrow our horizons, perpetuating a conservative status quo. This is why the "them" concept is generally promoted by those in power. However, the "them" created in one society sharpens the "us" in another, culminating in enmities that may become destructive.

If the Communists of the cold war era are today our friends, and if the US has been able to elect a black president, then solutions to the Israeli–Palestinian issue, or the rising Christian-Moslem antagonism must be sought by similarly eliminating the "us versus them" mindset.

EDUCATION AS THE KEY TO PEACE AND TOLERANCE

Clearly we must be able to go beyond these observations and wish lists to be able fill the gaps in our minds. The answers extend beyond individual and one-sided efforts, but are in a global education effort to lay the foundation of such changes in mindset. A review of education systems and books in different parts of the world, with such a purpose in mind, will enable peoples, brought ever closer together by developments in technology, to overcome their differences. The "us versus them" concept pushes us not to enlarge the pie but rather to concentrate on how we share it. If mankind were to concentrate on overcoming problems together, and in peace, quality of life would improve globally for all.

This thinking lies at the root of religions, which are intended to improve quality of life. We learn from the historical records that Mevlana Celaleddin-i Rumi (the Sufi religious leader, poet and thinker of the twelfth century) regularly visited the monasteries to exchange views with Christian and Jewish religious people. Prominent Christian clergymen came from Istanbul to discuss with him certain theological issues. It was Yunus Emre, the great Sufi poet and thinker of the thirteenth century, who preached in one of his poems: "Regard the other, as you regard yourself, this is the meaning of the four Holy Books, if there is any."

Overcoming the gaps in mindset is important to our global future. Take for example the instance of the European Union's approach to the membership of Turkiye, a subject discussed earlier in the book. To the surprise of many, after fifty years of courting, Turkiye successfully completed many reforms and secured negotiations for accession to the European Union. However, the recent developments in the negotiations is failing to create an impression of mutually trusting future partners, but is one of European reluctance to accept Turkiye as an equal partner.

Overcoming the "us versus them" mentality has significant economic gains for countries, companies, and individuals. One of the two important issues foremost in a CEO's mind is to attract talent; the other is to impact the structuring of his particular sector with mergers, acquisitions, or alliances.

When attracting talent, we should be able to reach into a pool of widely divergent people in terms of age, gender, nationality, religion or sexual preferences. Many countries are revising their immigration policies to attract qualified people regardless of the foregoing. We should not be afraid of people's backgrounds or history that they bring along with their qualifications, but rather take advantage of speaking to their differences.

The primary impediment to smooth and successful relationships between people, companies, and countries is cited as "cultural difference." It is true that culture is the real motivating force behind stability, but also of change. However, culture is not static, and it evolves within society. A resistance to change of culture is determined by existing structures of vested interests. Therefore, establishing new orders for vested interests and managing them is determinant in evolving cultures, and is a consideration of high importance for people in positions of power, whether of a country or a company.

DIVERSITY BREEDS RICHNESS

If we are to be successful in including rather than excluding all communities in global governance structures, we have to improve our ability to manage diversity. The past experiences of mankind can meaningfully contribute to the refinement of diversity management. Let's take the example of Turkiye. There is a depth of experience in managing diversity accumulated over centuries in Turkiye. For example, when we look at the history of the Ottoman and Anatolian civilizations what we see is a great fluidity between religions and communities. As an example, the Seljuk Sultan Izzeddin Keykavus II, whose mother was a descendant of the Byzantine aristocracy, routinely organized in his palace theological discussions between Christian priests and Muslim religious leaders. This tradition, particularly highlighted in its Sufi variant, embodies a philosophy of great tolerance and accommodation.

This tradition of accommodation and tolerance is the reason why until the late nineteenth century the Ottoman political order did not experience ethnic discrimination. What marked the Seljuk and Ottoman experience in this field was a very specific definition of the "self" and the "other" and an associated administrative form of social organization considerably different from that in the Western world. In this form of organization, the so-called "Millet" (Community) system, different communities enjoyed a considerably high level of autonomy. This system also allowed non-Muslims to be appointed to administrative positions that required a high level of political and financial trustworthiness.

In the nineteenth century the rise of race-based nationalism in the West had its echoes in the Ottoman territory as well. The course of events proceeded in a chain of reactions, paving the way to great sufferings in all parts of the society. Despite the inevitably irregular advance of history, the fundamental context of life in Anatolia is one of coexistence between different groups. In that sense Anatolia's legacy to the world is one of great diversity management full of rich experiences.

In the new millennium, success still requires sound management of diversity. The experiences of Turkiye have, therefore, the potential to make a significant contribution to the international process of furthering the progress towards better governance of the world.

BENEFITS OF THE INTERNET

Developments in information and communication technology increase the interdependency of people, institutions, and countries. People can easily access people with common interests in different parts of the world and establish intensive relationships with them. They sometimes even find their life partners in other corners of the world.

One individual can be part of several different networks. Therefore, he can both increase his knowledge in his professional and private life, and keep up to date. Some groups start up projects over the Internet; others organize protest movements that can influence government decisions.

Therefore the universe of the Internet opens up new worlds for us, as well as bringing about changes in our behavior. There are several different types of roles that people with successful applications of using the Internet adopt:

- Developmental – people that run these networks energize the participants, coach them through regular and constant feedback, and urge contributions from them. In this manner, they encourage sharing of information and experience, and increase the effectiveness of the net.
- Adaptive – these are used by people who take it upon themselves to cross fertilize the various networks that they are a part of, therefore enhancing all that they are part of.

- Researcher – these are people that take it upon themselves to research and respond to questions that come up in the Internet, and they become reference points.
- Intermediate – these are people that rather than research the answers themselves guide people to those that may have the answers, and motivate such answers, thereby increasing the fluidity of the net.
- Compiler – these people compile the contributions to the network, summarize them, and share them both within and outside the network. In this way, they increase and spread the influence of the network.
- Mentor – these are people that are expert in the specific area of the network and provide expert content. They share their ideas and guide the opinions or actions of the network participants.

Networks that have members with these different attributes develop faster and can be effective in society; therefore attracting members with these attributes has a bearing in the success of the network. As individuals, we have to be up to date in our approach and understanding of effectively using the Internet. Being effective and trustworthy members of the Internet enables us to increase our influence.

We must be individuals that believe in information sharing rather than keeping it to ourselves, that trust not only our immediate circle but go beyond that, that believe that we can create value in any part of the world by working together with others, that create our own solutions rather than expecting solutions from others. We must not be fatalistic but rather plan our future; we must learn to be accountable for our actions.

Ultimately, success in the web world belongs to inquisitive, research oriented, participative, partaking, communicative, self-starter people with a sense of responsibility. In order to prepare for the future as a society, we must revise our education systems and behavior accordingly.

EDUCATION REFORM TO ACHIEVE CULTURAL REFORM

The most efficient way to increase the quality of life is to increase the quality of governance. The key to increasing the quality of governance is to improve the quality of education in the society. Education improves the quality of life of not only the educated but also society. Therefore, the sufficient and proper education of young generations is the most assured way of increasing the welfare of a society.

Managing long-term cultural change is possible only through radical reform of the education system and its content. Improvements in the education system will not only facilitate mental transformation, but also improve competitiveness in the global arena. In order to be competitive, we must use our resources productively and effectively. Human resource is the most valuable resource we have. Public policy has a large role to play in this area. Endowment of future generations with a good education is the best way to invest in the future.

Better educated generations are progressively more efficient and productive and therefore are instrumental in improving overall welfare levels. Children of educated mothers are better educated, better motivated, in better health, and better overall in problem solving.

The level of education and population planning has a direct correlation. Therefore education is indirectly the antidote to poverty, since as the level of education increases, the tendency to plan financially for the future also increases, enabling a healthy financial balance between generations.

An educated society:

- adapts quickly to innovation and technology, and hence contributes to value added research and development investments;
- demands better goods and services, improving overall market development;
- has lower rates of crime, pointing to a safer and more secure lifestyle;
- has higher levels of volunteer work and charitable contributions, resulting in higher levels of social stability;
- makes conscious decisions with respect to social issues, increasing the quality of democracy.

Where so much is to be gained by society overall, education systems worldwide should aspire to bring up individuals that are modern in a new global sense. These are individuals with a competitive edge, inquisitive minds, with an ability to share, participate, communicate, and take the initiative, and to follow through with responsibility. The education system to generate such individuals should be designed not to upload and store information but rather to know how to reach information, and to stimulate creative thinking, which is the foundation of creating value.

The education system should have the following objectives of shaping the patterns of thinking and the lives of young people:

- **Develop critical thinking** so that they are able to evaluate events through considering different points of view rather than have a tendency to adopt views as presented to them, to analyze issues by breaking them down to components, and to generate new syntheses from the components.

- **Develop creative thinking** so that they are able to express themselves in different forms, to learn different languages, to have an open-mindedness about understanding other cultures, to accept diversity and differences as a richness rather than as factors to eliminate and sideline.
- **Develop communication skills** so that they are able to present ideas effectively, in order that the ideas can find support and applicability, to develop discussion skills, to be able to use audio and visual media to present their ideas, to develop new ideas with self-confidence.
- **Develop the ability to adapt to changing technology** so that they are able to follow the global agenda by integration in various networks, to pursue employment opportunities through the use of information technologies, and to be versatile with use of technology in order to maintain a competitive edge.
- **Develop the ability to use time efficiently** so that they can understand the importance of the use of time, and how the good use of such an equitably distributed resource can be used to promote success and advancement.
- **Develop global awareness and participation** so that they have the awareness of global issues such as protection of the environment, respect for human rights, and diversity, to work in election campaigns or on projects with people of different backgrounds, establishing strong foundations for global citizenship.
- **To be physically fit** and to have an understanding of the importance of healthy habits for themselves and for those around them, to develop athletic skills necessary for healthy body and team sports.

If the priority of such objectives can be adopted for the concept and process of education, young people will be learning in an environment of continuous self-development, looking for new ways of reaching knowledge, technology, thinking, and sharing. Therefore, the most important priority for an education system is providing content that promotes skill development.

Academic content as well as presentation should be up-to-date in terms of cases presented and relevant to the current global agenda. Developing critical thinking skills requires that ideas be presented with a pluralistic approach, integrating different points of view, and in a balanced manner taking into account global, national, or regional perspectives, thereby imparting a wide perspective.

Applied methods are more effective than theoretical education and promote independent learning abilities. Field assignments or experiments are more stimulating and instructional than pure classroom instruction.

Developing language and conceptualization abilities appropriate to the age group is also critical in increasing the effectiveness of education. Measuring and evaluation opportunities should be possible to enable self-evaluation and therefore provide motivation for improvement.

Interdisciplinary cross-references are also very useful in making learning multidimensional and effective. Providing references and citing sources in textbooks stimulates and encourages further learning.

The use of technology in schooling has benefits from both an access and a quality of content point of view. A lack of laboratory facilities in many schools around the world can be compensated for by virtual experiments conveyed over the Internet. If the Internet were to provide a medium where students can test themselves and identify specific learning needs, then it would be tantamount to a personally focused learning opportunity for all.

If a historical content for current global events were to be provided and be made available through the Internet, it would serve to increase the interest in these events, and therefore stimulate the willingness to contribute to solutions of global issues.

Education systems should encourage analytical and critical thinking and deemphasize testing of learning through examinations alone. Universities should be pillars of knowledge creation.

EVOLUTION OF SOCIAL BEHAVIOR

When we think of life as a whole, we should not only understand the interrelationships between various segments of society, but also consider the interdependencies. We should try to place our lives in the context of the world, and think about what out contributions could be. The world is evolving in such a way that all values are becoming global, and developments in information technology are eroding borders. Global integration is increasing our responsibility to overcome the big challenge of aligning our social values and behavior.

The primary reason behind the global terror threats and wars in various parts of the world is the sharpening social behavior of different peoples. As long as these differences are not reconciled, there will continue to be terrorist acts, wars, and massacres.

Global issue have a large impact on our daily lives, this will be even truer for the lives of our children. We must therefore try to achieve a mental transformation in embracing global values, and internalize them as far as possible. We must be cognizant that all our actions have far reaching consequences.

Genetically modified seeds in one part of the world impact on indigenous farming in another, excessive hunting in a certain area disrupts immigration patterns of animals, impacting on another area, destruction of rain forests by excessive logging in South America or overuse of elements that harm the ozone layer in North America leads to oxygen imbalances globally.

The increase in world population to eight billion from five billion and pollution leads to water shortages, inability to prevent soil erosion and poor irrigation practices on agricultural land exacerbates the global hunger problem.

SOCIAL ISSUES THREATEN GLOBAL PEACE

Our global issues extend far beyond those of the environment. Societal issues have consequences just as serious. Oppression or marginalization of those with different convictions or opinions leads to issues that threaten global peace. While borders may present an impediment to working together, organized crime or terrorist networks take advantage of developments in global technology to work together.

Imbalances on earth are another big threat to global peace. About one-fifth of people living on earth are trying to survive on US$1 a day income, and nearly half of them manage on US$2 a day. Developed countries spend US$600 billion on military expenditures; provide agricultural subsidies of around US$300 billion, while their foreign aid budgets do not total to US$60 billion. Furthermore the proportion of humans living in developed countries is decreasing every year.

WE SHOULD ALL BE "A CITIZEN OF THE WORLD"

In the past two decades, income distribution between developed and undeveloped countries has become distorted. While on the one hand institutions worldwide are becoming more global, rules of the game differ widely between countries. The inconsistencies in rules governing genetic engineering, biotechnology, e-trade, competition, or taxation render rules impractical. There is no system for sharing the riches of the oceans or space equitably, when these should rightfully be shared by all.

TOLERANCE AND HARMONY CAN SOLVE
SOCIAL ISSUES

In summary, as topics about our daily life gain global characteristics, our vision, organizations, and management systems should also gain a global perspective. As the world becomes more interconnected, we have to understand that the problems of others are also our own. Therefore, we have to make sure that good governance principles are applied throughout our management structures and systems.

Good governance is in fact "self-governance." It means freeing ourselves of our fears, opening up our eyes, hearts, and minds to new perspectives, and adopting tolerance. It means wishing for others what we would wish for ourselves.

Management concepts have evolved to include reciprocity, participation, and transparency to become "governance" concepts. This is the concept of the modern age, and the basis of human rights and democracy.

A major prerequisite to this participative management approach is that large masses are interested in the developments that impact their lives, have the necessary information, and possess the tools to participate in decision making. To this end, they must belong to the information age and access information technologies. It is a global responsibility to take the necessary steps to satisfy these needs. It is an overarching responsibility that crosses national boundaries, one to be assumed by the international community as a whole.

For sustainable development and world peace, we must have a good grasp of how our decisions affect others, and attain the wisdom to be unselfish about these decisions. Politicians, NGOs, and individuals all have important roles to play in these undertakings. Enabling people to take part in global decision making processes that will ultimately affect them and hence shape their future is fundamental to the modern age.

DEMOCRACY MUST BE STRENGTHENED
BY PARTICIPATION

In the earliest stages of democracy, only certain citizens could vote. Decisions regarding the society would be voted on by those vested with the right to vote. This concept of "participation" in democracy was eventually replaced by "representation," as a result of increasing population, increasing number of decisions, and complexity of these decisions. Today, with the exception of the Swiss example, democracies are representative democracies.

However, the interests of the representatives and the people they represent may not always be congruent, what the economists call, the "agency problem." Societies made more discerning by education and information technology want to have more say in their government. The gravity of decisions and the developments in the twenty-first century point to a need for participative democracy.

The global decision making mechanisms today cannot be said to be very democratic. Countries have voting powers that are determined by factors beyond the size of their populations. For example, it is difficult to justify the lack of veto power for India at the United Nations when France has one, regardless of which criteria is utilized: number of citizens, economic might, or being a nuclear power. Greece can have more of a bearing on decisions than India by virtue of the fact that it is an EU member. The current system is a relic of history that needs to be adapted to twenty-first century realities.

On the other hand, can the world accept the "one man – one vote" principle, that is the practice within national boundaries, to also be applied in global affairs? Would this bring global legitimacy? Or, should each country's vote be equal on global system regardless of its size? Or, should countries be able to vote according to their military power? Or should governments and/or companies and/or people be given voting rights according to their economic weights? In that case, how should changes in these weights over time be managed in order to secure the legitimacy of a global system?

Human rights are traditionally based on the principles of no individual being discriminated against on the basis of gender, color, race, language, religion, social class, or political beliefs. Democracy is traditionally based on the right to vote, and freedom of belief, thought, speech and assembly.

Today these traditional definitions need to be expanded to include the participation of people in the global decision making processes shaping their own future. This transformation lies at the heart of the change of focus from management to governance, emphasizing participation and mutuality.

If decision makers miss the importance of this transformation, success in public policy making will be increasingly difficult because civil society organizations which are instrumental in shaping the standards, in the gathering and dissemination of the information that feeds decision making, problem solving, are also compelling participatory democracy. This is not to say civil society organizations are looking to replace elected representatives or public institutions, but that they are more vigilant to challenge them in order to support and improve their functioning in a participatory manner.

CURRICULUM FOR GLOBAL CITIZENSHIP

To correct the imbalances in the world in a sustainable way, we must be interested in the problems of others and feel the responsibility to help others. The fact that other people's problems will come to be our problems if not sorted does not seem to sink in.

When we look at education curricula around the world, we see that these are more based on nationalist notions emphasizing discriminatory thinking, and have no dimension of "world citizenship." As Einstein put it, "Nationalism is a childhood disease. It is the measles of humanity." Therefore the remedy will have to be applied at a young age.

If we are to solve the issues relevant to the future of human kind, and if we really believe in human rights and democracy, we should strive for the education and bringing up of all people of this earth to instill the "world citizen" notion and their participation in decision making processes.

Going beyond formal education years, people should continue to take an active part in civil society organizations and interact internationally through civil society organizations. The public sector, on the other hand, should view civil society organizations not as nuisances or competitors, but rather as means to enable participation and improve transparency and accountability.

If we truly believe in human rights and democracy, we must strive to get our future generations educated with the notion of "global citizenship" and contribute to decision making processes with this view. If we are successful in fighting ignorance, we will be more successful than we ever were about fighting poverty and achieving peace and prosperity.

Conclusion

In a world where interdependence between societies is gaining more and more recognition, a functioning global democracy is only possible if individuals have the ability to have a say in their future and are able to participate in global decision making processes. This is the new age definition of human rights and democracy. One of the major prerequisites of such participative democracy is for the masses to have an interest in the events that impact their lives, and on having such an interest, to have the means and access to information. Enabling this is a global responsibility beyond that of any single country. However, currently the curricula of many national education systems focus on nation building, with an insufficient emphasis on global citizenship.

Therefore, a global education initiative aimed at increasing the quality of education in order to improve the level of global peace and welfare should be developed, to ensure that people fully understand their mutual dependence, rather than seeing neighbors and other foreigners as scapegoats for local problems. Living together requires sharing power – whether in the family, in the village, in the city, in a nation, or in the world. Only after this is established can we create global institutions with adequate resources and decision-making powers that are shared and exercised equitably.

One of the major prerequisites to achieving global education reform is to redefine our global priorities, to place the education of large masses of people as global citizens at the top of the agenda, and to agree on general guidelines of how and what we will teach young people.

The second is to provide large numbers of people with the necessary means that would make them interested in and adequately informed about the affairs that influence their lives. This requires the right to have an access to education and information technology, that is, an equitable and fair distribution of such means. Unless an equitable access to knowledge and means of communication among the people of the world can be provided, there cannot be a world free of discrimination, prejudice, and animosity.

A lack of appropriate infrastructure and the lack of education to participate in the new world of the "connected society" present serious threats to establishing new governance structures based on the principles of democracy and equality. For the "connected society" the focus of exchanges in a wide range of fields from economy and politics to culture and social life is shifting from the real to the virtual sphere. Patterns of life, work, and sharing relationships are also undergoing radical changes. At the same time, those who are unable to catch up with this revolution are being left outside the system at an alarming rate. This development presents the danger of an alienated two-tier society in contrast to the exciting prospect of efficient governance patterns based on the principles of democracy and equity.

If there is no adequate grasp of the importance of education in arriving at good governance patterns, humanity will be shaken at the global scale, by the fault line between the enlightened and the ignorant. This fault line differs from the geological ones in that it is in the minds of people, the most valuable and important medium, where it is more difficult to observe and far more difficult to repair.

Shaping the Future of a Nation – Turkiye: Cradle of Civilizations, Land of Inspiration, and a Catalyst for Peace

Love and knowledge increase when shared.

'Ultimate origin of all phenomena is change.' (Fou-Hi)

To turn Turkiye into a globally highly regarded country where all its citizens view their future with confidence, and one that has high international competitive capacity, there must be a resolutely pursued concept and action plan. The target of achieving certain established standards is not enough, what needs to be done is to establish and meet new and more challenging standards. Otherwise it is possible to fall behind evolving standards. As an example, with reference to the ongoing EU membership talks for Turkiye, the question has to be not what criteria to achieve and when, but rather what it is that Turkiye can add to the criteria to lead Europe to new and higher standards. The issue to focus on can be defined as contributing to Europe as a European, and then this point of view is the first step to shaping the future of Europe that Turkiye wants to be part of. One such aspiration could be "A European Union that becomes a role model for global governance."

FORMULATING THE VISION

Turkiye is currently being defined as a country of "regional power," "a global player," "strategic partner," "role model," "Trojan horse of the west," "moderate Islamic country," secular Islamic country," "balancing country," and "bridge country" by various parties. How should Turkiye define its own role and what kind of vision should it have?

Turkiye sits at a point where various dynamics are at work. To make the most of this position, the country must formulate a global vision both at government and citizen level, and not remain inward looking. If the citizens, state, and private and non-profit institutions of a country can take the steps to agree on a vision for the future then the country has the potential to shape its own future.

Turkiye can be positioned as a production center for Europe, as a place for quality retirement, as a crossroads for energy resource diversification, as an economic engine for the Middle East, as a gateway to Central Asian resources, and as a country with the intellectual potential to address global issues.

As an example, the planning of educational need should take into account not just Turkiye's requirements but also those of the geographic region surrounding it. Many countries surrounding Turkiye, for example, the Ukraine, Russia and those in the European Union have aging populations. As a result the medical requirements of these countries will increase. If Turkiye takes this into consideration when planning it educational strategy it will be able to provide more places for medical and support staff training as well as increase a focus on the languages that will be required.

The important point is to be able to extend the vision behind the planning beyond Turkish borders. If Turkish business people, public sector managers, and individuals adopt a global point of view then Turkiye will be able to add value beyond its borders. If a country can offer solutions to global issues and hence create value, it also takes strides in increasing its own welfare and power.

ACCESSING GLOBAL RESOURCES

To achieve its vision, Turkiye needs resources. Domestic resources alone are insufficient to realize the country's potential, and Turkiye has to access international markets in order to borrow to finance growth. It has to compete with other emerging markets when attracting foreign investment.

In a global order where it has become critical for countries to extend their field of economic influence, Turkiye has to increase its access to global resources by increasing its competitiveness. The welfare and reputation of a country are enhanced by its global competitiveness. A country that adheres to consistent principles and therefore attains strength is globally successful in other areas as well. Therefore increasing competitiveness should be one major target to increase Turkiye's sphere of influence.

The other is to increase the mind share of Turkiye. Compelling yet realistic themes have to be developed for this purpose, and followed up consistently to maintain credibility.

One of the most critical resources for development is intellectual power. Therefore, recruiting those who can make a difference in the intellectual sphere is key to development.

INCREASING COMPETITIVENESS

To increase global competitiveness, a country needs a mental transformation: every individual and every institution has to direct its economic activity to maximize productivity, meet their respective social responsibilities, and invest in technology, information, and innovation. The labor market should be flexible enough for competitiveness, and investment should be concentrated in value added areas. Atatürk once famously said and quoted: "Nations that have made a habit of seeking a comfortable living without working hard or learning are bound to lose first their dignity, then their identity, then their freedom."

Qualified employment in the public sector is a major determinant in increasing productivity, as is battling corruption. Increasing tax collection and reducing the size of the unregistered economy are also important in improving competitiveness.

The most basic input for a country's development is its intellectual capital. Action has its origins in thought. Individuals and people who do not think and create for themselves have to work for a future that others have designed. Therefore, providing incentives for original content, policy, and intellectual development is the key to accessing global resources more effectively. Investing in education and allocating more resources for research and development are therefore other important areas of emphasis when aiming to increase competitiveness.

DEVELOPING THE TURKIYE BRAND

Information technology is instrumental in rapid dissemination of ever growing amounts of information. Therefore, people are constantly under bombardment from information against which they have to develop a selective perception. Every type of product is therefore competing with products outside its own category as well. The reason for this competition is not only increasing market share but also increasing "mind share." Attracting people's attention additionally requires a mind share associated with the country of origin. Brand value of a country has an indirect influence on all the products derived in that country, highlighting a critical feature.

Exports from Turkiye are growing faster than its growth rate. This is a sign that its share and role in the global economy is increasing.

However, the value added of exports is not increasing at the same rate. The same product produced in Germany can sell for more than the product with exactly the same specifications when produced in Turkiye. This indicates that the brand value of a country has an impact on the value it derives from global markets and therefore on its overall welfare level. The most valuable foreign capital is the value added gained from exports of products and services.

As an example, Germany can command a higher value for engineering related goods or services because of the higher value people place on such by association with Germany. Technology is associated with the US. China is associated with low cost production. Finland has attained a good mind share due to Nokia. Hence, it is fair to say that countries can differentiate themselves by how they are perceived. These perceptions have an impact on their economies. The country of origin carries a message everywhere in the world. If for instance Turkiye were able to command a higher brand value of only 5%, this translates into more than five billion dollars higher value added annually. This means the most effective resource is the foreign capital created by such value added in exports. Increasing Turkiye's brand value is a matter of increasing its prosperity and is not only a matter for the state.

Evaluating Turkiye for its brand recognition shows that its perception is very different from reality. A good indicator in this regard is the reaction of people that visit for the first time: 95% say that their impressions are surprisingly positive, meaning that their prior expectations and realized experience are seriously different. This would imply that Turkiye is poor in its public relations. In the global public opinion, the perception about Turkish companies or Turkish goods or services is not one of enthusiasm, and lags far behind reality.

Branding should be viewed not as a matter of publicity, but rather as a matter of strategy. Promotion, positioning, and branding must all be considered within the context of the targets to be achieved. To position Turkiye as a brand needs a conceptual framework. Some principles need to be observed in developing this. First is the philosopher Mevlana's principle of "Be as you seem, seem as who you are." An identity that does not inherently reflect Turkiye cannot be successful. The Turkiye brand needs to be built on values that are actually exercised in Turkiye. Second, as Turkiye is a multifaceted country it is not possible to put forth all aspects. The choice aspects should have the potential to add value. The aspects put forward should be unique to Turkiye and thus add value.

Some unique aspects for Turkiye that can be utilized are discussed below.

TURKIYE AS A PRODUCTION CENTER FOR THE EU

High labor costs in the EU and an aging population have the impact of shifting production centers to Turkiye, as can be observed in automotive, and white and brown goods sectors. Turkiye has the advantage of a young, hard-working, dynamic, and qualified work force that has similar working practices to the EU. To make Turkiye a production center for the EU requires going beyond having the highest number of quality awards to giving priority to vocational training, identifying and focusing on the needs of European customers, and inspiring all institutions of the country to high achievement. This will also facilitate technological development and increase foreign capital.

THE EU NEEDS TURKIYE

Growth rates of Turkiye since 2001 have been the highest in the OECD area. What is different from the past is the fact that in the period since 2001, Turkiye has carried out some of the most impressive and long-awaited structural reforms, which were recognized by the international community: the EU has agreed to open full membership negotiations with Turkiye and the IMF declared Turkiye a success story. It would not be an exaggeration to suggest that in the absence of a force majeure, Turkiye is set on the right track for sustainable economic growth of satisfactory levels.

Furthermore, the long-term perspectives look even more promising. With Turkish population growth rate having fallen from over 2% to 1.5%, it is on the verge of entering a "golden demographic period" similar to that experienced by East Asia in the 1980s, where the productive working population is the largest section of society, thus providing the potential for even more rapid income growth.

This situation is likely to be a panacea for improving European competitiveness as well as Turkish competitiveness. The continuation of reforms to bring Turkiye into full EU membership will not only increase the confidence in the Turkish potential and investments in Turkiye, but is also likely to make Turkiye indispensable to the EU.

Only a few emerging markets in the world have the potential of attracting investment both for export as well as for their domestic market. Turkiye is in a privileged position to create a **virtuous investment cycle**, with a more competitive domestic business environment further strengthening Turkiye as a platform for exports, and exports in turn stimulating firms to upgrade and serve the domestic market more efficiently. This is true not only for products, but also for the young managers. Young Turks are being employed by global firms throughout the world, with their professionalism and flexibility to deal with a wide range of circumstances. The Chairman of Pfizer once suggested to me that the most important export of their Turkish operation is that of qualified managers/leaders . The CEO of Coca-Cola, Muhtar Kent, is a case in point.

Recently, Turkiye has become one of the top countries to be European Quality Award winners, and Turkish brands are becoming household names in a wide range of countries. In short, with high growth potential, a qualified workforce and managers, and the entrepreneurial spirit, Turkiye provides an important potential market for global businesses. Furthermore, regional political stability can only be established on a sustainable basis if the economic development spreads throughout the region. The engine for growth in the Balkans, Caucuses, Central Asia, and the Middle East is likely to be Turkiye. Perhaps most importantly, as an observer of the Turkish economy has put it, "Turkiye will be the 'viagra' for Europe" by becoming the key agent in improving European competitiveness.[1]

COMMERCIAL, FINANCIAL, AND CULTURAL CENTER FOR THE MIDDLE EAST, CAUCUSES, AND THE BALKANS

Turkiye is at the centre of the economic and political area known as "Eurasia," where three regions of the world, Europe, the former Soviet Union, and the Middle East intersect. The proximity to the Balkans and the rest of Europe as well as to the growing emerging markets in Central Asia, the Middle East, and North Africa creates unique business opportunities. The experience of numerous global firms confirms Turkiye as a predominant investment location and export platform. Companies like Microsoft, Coca-Cola, GE, Procter & Gamble, and Phillip Morris, as well as international investment institutions like the World Bank Group's International Finance Corporation have already selected Turkiye as a regional base. Turkiye is fast becoming a "production centre for Europe" in diverse industries, but in particular in automotives.

Turkiye is also the leading investor in the Caucasian and Central Asian Turkic Republics. Due to strong cultural and historic ties, Turkiye provides privileged access and a sound base to develop business with these countries.

The international perception of Turkiye in terms of a destination for investment is generally shaped by the diverse market opportunities, both domestic and export-oriented, it is able to offer. The potential of these markets covers over one billion consumers.

Turkiye should direct its economic policies to support the move of these neighboring countries toward democracy and market economies. Economic development of Iraq, Syria, Georgia, and Armenia can all be facilitated by Turkiye's involvement and experience in such an economic transformation. Turkiye can develop distribution channels, logistical support, and branding abilities in the region.

Economic relations with Russia and Iran also have the potential to reflect positively on security and politics in the region. Approaching the Middle East peace process constructively with a view to what Turkiye can add to the process is of strategic importance. Development and sustainability of economic development is a major contributor to a lasting peace in the region. The key to economic development is not aid, but trade.

As an example, perhaps a major contribution that the US can make to a sustainable peace in the region is to expand the free trade agreement in force with Israel to other countries in the region. Turkiye should lobby to introduce this as an option and to benefit from it.

PEACE AT HOME AND PEACE IN THE WORLD

The "zero conflicts" policy that Turkiye is pursuing with its neighbors increases the respect and credibility it commands. Turkiye's stance in the Iraqi conflict is a testament that it does not have any expansionary designs in the region. The contribution by the Turkish army in Somali, Afghanistan, and Bosnia has enhanced Turkiye's strong and just image.

When Turkiye adopts a just, win–win attitude to foreign policy development and becomes a player that generates initiatives for peace, it carries "Peace in the World" to a context that is beyond simply non-aggression. Approaching water use from Tigres and Euphrates rivers to one of basin management jointly with Syria and Iraq, creating solutions with Greece over the Aegean disputes, and taking initiatives jointly with Russia and the Central Asian countries over energy logistics all position Turkiye as a country that seeks preventive solutions to potential economic conflicts. Turkish efforts in the positive outcome of the 2004 referendum in Cyprus over reunification have served to highlight Turkiye's conciliatory approach. This has lifted the major impediment to the start of membership negotiations between Turkiye and the EU, a credit to Turkish diplomatic policy. Unfortunately, however, it was not reciprocated in the conclusion over the Cyprus issue. Furthermore, EU did not honor its promises to the Turkish Cypriots.

HISTORY, CULTURE, DIVERSITY, THE YOUNG, AND THE OLD

Turkiye has a growing tourism sector. However, this sector creates a lot less value added than its potential. There must be better publicity to draw attention to the fact that Turkiye has many sacred sites of early Christianity; Troy and Mesopotamia; has been the cradle of many civilizations; Istanbul has been the capital of many empires and many other cultures have flourished in the land. These should be brought to the attention of potential tourists. This would add more value to tourism revenues and would promote this cultural vision throughout the world.

Today intellectual capital is more important than financial capital. Leading countries make up for their deficiencies in creative and informed brainpower by luring such individuals from other countries. Turkiye should aim to attract not only foreign financial capital, but also foreign intellectual capital.

Turkiye's cultural and historical legacy can be a competitive advantage as well. 500 years ago Turkiye hosted the victims of the Spanish Inquisition. Mehmet the Conqueror granted many rights to members of different religious and cultural communities after the conquest of Istanbul. These, along with Turkiye's reputation for generous hospitality are testimony to her ability and experience to live with diversity. As xenophobia makes a comeback in several European countries, Turkiye provides an attractive alternative workplace for foreigners.

Turkiye's mild Mediterranean climate, natural and historical riches are not just tourist attractions. They also attest to a high quality of living. Istanbul has become one of the most exciting cities in Europe when it comes to nightlife. The fact that it is a desirable place to live is behind the decisions of many companies to move their regional headquarters to Istanbul. Preferences of the young determine the trends in the world. Attracting them can turn Turkiye into a trendsetting country.

Turkiye can also become a retirement destination with its mild climate and good medical care. Well-educated medical staff and service experience from the tourism sector can complement the climate and produce a desirable place to live for aging Europeans with the potential of it becoming the Florida of the EU. This addresses the issue of care of the aging population in the EU while contributing to Turkiye's economic growth.

SILICON VALLEY OF EUROPE

Prior to September 11, the number of work permits and citizenships issued by the US to experts in Information Technology (IT) had doubled in the two preceding years. Microsoft's research indicates that despite heavy investment in education Europe's deficit in its IT workforce will increase from 8% to 14%. Germany is preparing its largest program since the 1970s to attract foreigners to work in the IT sector.

Since Turkiye devotes limited resources to research and development, it needs to be able to attract as much brainpower as financial capital. Since information sharing contributes to faster development, industries that rely on information and technologies like to congregate in clusters. During World War II, German academics fleeing Hitler's regime made great contributions to the development of science and the university system in Turkiye. If Turkiye can provide the necessary infrastructure and proper incentives for creative minds and attract them then this will help the development of the country and its people.

The attraction of creative minds deserves equal and perhaps higher priority than attracting foreign capital and thus it should become a state policy. If Turkiye becomes a world center of development in information and ideas, then Turkiye can look forward to a more prosperous future.

The twenty-first century vision of Turkiye as a quality place to live and generate ideas is a good starting point for further economic and social development. The quality of life improves with the quality of the people that one lives with.

These themes can also be the key to overcome some established prejudices regarding Turkiye. If Turkiye is positioned around themes that are realistic, striking, and consistent in content and communication, then access to world resources will become easier.

RELATIONS WITH THE US

The relations between Turkiye and the United States are based on common values and ideals with regard to democracy, freedom, human rights, and free market economy. Turks and Americans are so committed to these values and ideals that they did not hesitate to fight together in Korea. It was the same ideals that fueled cooperation in Bosnia, Somalia, and Afghanistan, and that led to Turkiye's perception as a strategic ally by the various administrations and the US military.

The strength of various minority lobbies in US politics has from time to time impacted on the US Congress' decisions or attitudes adversely with respect to Turkiye and relationships have suffered setbacks due to differences of interests and priorities. For example, the differences that led to the 1964 Johnson Letter arms embargo in the period 1975–1978, and the differences in the priorities in the operations conducted in northern Iraq led to some tensions between the two countries.

However, these tensions do not negate the devotion of the two peoples to the same ideals, and those differences are overcome in one way or another. The foundation of the relations between Turkiye and the United States remains sound.

After September 11, the US has been more sensitive to global threats and inclined to use its technological and military might to influence world order. To this end, the US has taken the position of "those who are not with us are against us," and not refrained from straining relationships with countries previously in alliance with them. However, it has become clear that where reciprocal economic relations impact many institutions and companies, the relationships healed in a speedy manner. This period has shown that developing mutual, intense, widespread and high volume commercial and trade relations can have an impact on political relations.

It is therefore important to increase the number of players and diversify the cultural and commercial relations between Turkiye and the US. The US economy is bigger than the EU economy, yet Turkiye's volume of trade with the EU is almost five times that of its volume of trade with the US, and this cannot necessarily be explained only by the proximity of the EU, given that the trade volume of Israel with the US is more than that of its trade volume with the EU by about 30%.

Turkiye has a trade deficit with the US, a rare position for US trading partners. It should be possible to benefit from the potential of the US economy by lifting the impediments to trade and Turkish companies putting the requisite emphasis on developing the US market.

Turkiye's position as the only secular and democratically governed Muslim country, its experience in fighting terror, and its military prowess make for a reliable ally and put it in a special position to enhance the strategic vision of promoting democracy, freedom, and a liberal economy. The US is also cognizant of this and is amenable to closer cooperation, paving the way for further developing economic and commercial ties.

Such cooperation will be effective if it extends the depth and breadth of the relationship with the US. A prosperous Turkiye will not only be the engine of growth and stability in the Middle East, but will also help the competitiveness of Europe, and the Atlantic partnership. US support for Turkiye's EU membership has been a very positive step in this direction.

When US President Barack Obama visited Ankara in 2009, it reinforced the idea that Turkiye is a role model for predominantly Muslim countries. A modern manufacturing economy with an information technology base; world-class managerial talent; and located at the crossroads of Europe and the Middle East, Turkiye has the potential to emerge as a regional powerhouse. During his visit to Turkiye, President Obama sent three critical messages:

1. He emphasized Turkiye's European credentials and secular character, as defined by the modern state's founder, Mustafa Kemal Atatürk. In doing so, Mr. Obama rebalanced the previous US view of Turkiye as a "moderate Islam" state. He said that he had chosen to visit Turkiye to send a message to the world. "Turkey is a critical ally. Turkey is an important part of Europe and Turkey and the United States must stand together and work together to overcome the challenges of our times."

2. He sent a key message to the Muslim world. He said "The United States is not, and will never be, at war with Islam." He also praised Islam's contribution to civilization and said America's relationship with it must extend beyond fighting terrorism. Speaking out on this from Turkiye reinforces the frequently articulated view of Turkiye as a bridge between civilizations that is capable of preventing conflict.

3. He sent a key message to Europe. Mr. Obama reiterated US support for Turkiye's EU membership, saying "Europe gains by the diversity of ethnicity, culture and faith – it is not diminished by it. And Turkish membership would broaden and strengthen Europe's foundation once more."

President Obama's support for Turkiye's EU membership bid is important, not only for Turkiye, but also for the EU. To the surprise of many, Turkiye successfully completed many reforms and secured negotiations for accession to the European Union. However, recent developments in Europe have created an impression that Europe is reluctant to accept Turkiye as an equal partner. Unless this changes, it will be difficult for Turkiye to proceed with its application for EU membership. This process will turn into one side constantly changing the goalposts and the other feeling alienated.

Yet, Europe and Turkiye have before them a historic opportunity to throw out the prejudices of the ages, discredit the clash of civilizations, and establish a stronger EU. Turkiye's membership has the potential to mitigate some of the key risks for Europe and help the EU become a role model for global governance.

THE SEARCH FOR TOMORROW

A search conference whose participants included key ministers from the government, leading representatives from the business world and academia, as well as economists, foreign policy specialists, opinion leaders, retired generals, and scientists were exposed to numerous potential scenarios for the future and were asked what priorities Turkiye has to follow under different scenarios about EU and US relations, peace versus continued tensions in the Middle East, and speed of economic activity shifting to different pillars.[2]

The purpose of the meeting was to identify and highlight critical issues for the next 20 years and also determine the steps that should be focused on in order to impact the future. Interestingly enough there were many common themes regardless of the scenarios: the following main points arose for Turkiye to concentrate on in order to actively manage her future:

- Turkiye should establish good governance principles in all its institutions.
- Turkiye should mobilize its educational resources to increase the technological and scientific effectiveness of its young population.
- Turkiye should enact a wide scope reform of her legal system.
- A strong economy is the true key to security. Therefore, the public sector, the private sector, NGOs and universities should cooperate and develop R&D and technology focused on generating high value added. Turkiye should actively focus on becoming the production center for the EU and service and commerce center for the region.
- Turkiye should establish balanced relations with the West and the countries within its region with respect to politics, commerce, energy dependence, use of water resources, and technological and defense cooperation. However, care should be taken to keep up with the developed world with respect to democracy, human rights, and liberal economic policies. Turkiye should take care to be an example in the region and take an active part in the shaping of the region.
- Turkiye should focus on developing the "Turkiye brand." To this end, Turkiye should make concerted efforts to develop relationships with Turks living abroad and other identified target groups to increase the value of the brand.
- Turkiye should develop the capability for long-term and strategic thinking in all its institutions.

In this regard, Turkiye is becoming a role model for global collaboration. Turkiye was recently chosen to serve on the UN Security Council gaining 80% of the votes in a secret ballot and has become a key intermediary in resolving numerous international conflicts in the Caucasus, Middle East, Eastern Europe, and Central Asia.

Along with Spain, Turkiye has also initiated The Alliance of Civilizations Project under the aegis of the United Nations. Its goal is to remedy the perceived "clash of civilizations" in international affairs. 'Zero problems with neighbors" policy of the Minister of Foreign Affairs of Turkiye, Ahmet Davutoğlu is a contemporary version of the vision of the founder of the country, Atatürk's dictum "Peace at home, peace in the world."

In short, Turkiye can focus on branding itself around the idea of "Türkiye: Cradle of Civilizations, Land of Inspiration, and a Catalyst for Peace" in a credible fashion.

If successful, such a branding would add value to the country.

NOTES

1 Comment made by Kalypso Nicolaidis, a member of EU Reflection Group, at a meeting in 2010 with Turkiye's State Minister and Chief Negotiator (Dogan Haber Ajansi) for the European Union, in Istanbul.
2 The conference was organized by ARGE Consulting and New Media Company jointly and invited not only international political experts, but also scientists from such leading institutions as MIT and Harvard University.

Suggested Reading

Adaman, F. and Çarkoğlu, A. 2000. *Türkiye'de Yerel ve Merkezi Yönetimlerde Hizmetlerden Tatmin, Patronaj İlişkileri ve Reform* (Istanbul: TESEV).

Addair, J. 1983. *Effective Leadership* (Aldershot: Gower).

Addair, J. 1986. *Effective Teambuilding* (Aldershot: Gower).

Ansoff, H.I. 1965. *Corporate Strategy* (New York: McGraw-Hill).

Ansoff, H.I. 1969. *Business Strategy* (Harmondsworth: Penguin Books).

Ansoff, H.I. 1976. *From Strategic Planning to Strategic Management* (with R. Hays and R. Declerck) (New York and London: John Wiley).

Ansoff, H.I. 1984, 1990. *Implanting Strategic Management* (Englewood Cliffs, NJ: Prentice-Hall).

Argüden, Y. and ARGE 2002. *Kurumsal Sosyal Sorumluluk* (Istanbul: Rota Yayin Yapim Tanitim).

Argüden, Y. ARGE, and Danışmanlık A.Ş. 2003. *İtibar Yönetimi* (Istanbul: BZD Yayinlari).

Argüden, Y. 2009. *Opportunity from Crisis: Obama's Chance for Real Global Leadership.* (Washington D.C.: The Globalist).

Argüden, Y. 2009. *From Global Crises to Global Governance.* (Washington D.C.: The Globalist).

Argüden, Y. 2009. *Boardroom Secrets: Corporate Governance for Quality of Life* (Basingstoke: Palgrave Macmillan).

Argüden, Y. 2009. *Consensual Delegation of Sovereignty.* (Washington D.C.: The Globalist).

Argüden, Y. 2010. *Diversity at the Head Table*, Global Corporate Governance Forum, *Private Sector Opinion*, 19.

Argüden, Y. 2010 *Measuring Effectiveness of Corporate Governance* (Fontainebleau: Insead).

Argyris, C. 1965. *Organization and Innovation* (Toronto: Irwin).

Atiyas, İ. 2000. *Devletin Düzenleyici Rolü* (TESEV).

Balı, A.Ş. 2001. *Çokkültürlülük ve Sosyal Adalet, 'Öteki' ile Barış İçinde Yaşamak* (Konya: Çizgi Kitabevi yayinlari).

Barnard, C. 1938. *The Functions of the Executive* (Cambridge, MA: Harvard University Press).

Barnard, C. 1948. *Organization and Management* (Cambridge, MA: Harvard University Press).

Baum, W.C. and Tolbert, S.M. 1985. *Investing in Development: Lessons of World Bank Experience* (New York: Oxford University Press).

Bennis, W. and Nanus, B. 1985. *Leaders: the Strategies for Taking Charge* (New York: Harper & Row).

Boztekin, N. 2004. *AB Uyum Süreci ve STK'lar*, (Istanbul: Tarih Vakfı Yayınları).

Buzan, T. 2000. *Mind Mapping* (New York: Plume Books).

Çakmak, A. 2003. *Düşünen Sivil Toplum: Felsefi Yaklaşımlar-Açılımlar* (Istanbul: Tarih Vakfi Yayınlari).Carnegie, Dale. 1987. *Dost Kazanma ve Insanları Etkileme Sanatı* (Istanbul: Yaprak Yayinlari).

Çarkoğlu, A. 2000. *Siyasi Partilerde Reform* (Istanbul: TESEV).

Collins, J. 2004. *İyi'den 'Mükemmel' Şirkete – Kalıcı Başarıya Ulaşmanın Yolları* (Boyner: Yayinlari).

Collins, J. 2002. *Built to Last* (New York: Harper Business).

Courtney, Hh. 2001. *2020 Foresight: Crafting Strategy in an Uncertain World* (Boston, MA: Harvard Business School Press).

Covey, S.R. 1992. *Principle Centered Leadership* (New York: Free Press).

Covey, S.R. 1998. *Önemli İşlere Öncelik* (Istanbul: Varlik Yayinlari).

Covey, S.R. 1998. *Seven Habits of Successful People*, (West Valley City, UT: Franklin Covey).

Chandler, A.D. 1962. *Strategy and Structure* (Cambridge, MA: MIT Press).

Chandler, A.D. 1977. *The Visible Hand: The Managerial Revolution in American Business* (Cambridge, MA: Harvard University Press).

Christensen, Clayton M. 1997. *The Innovator's Dilemma* (Boston, MA: Harvard Business School Press).

De Bono, E. 1982. *Lateral Thinking for Management* (Maidenhead: McGraw-Hill).

De Bono, E. 1985. *Six Thinking Hats* (London: Penguin).

De Bono, E. 1990. *I Am Right, You Are Wrong* (London: Viking).

Diamond, J. 1999. *Guns, Germs, and Steel: The Fates of Human Societies* (New York: Norton).

Dilmaç, B. 2002. *İnsanca Değerler Eğitimi* (Ankara: Nobel Yayın Dağitim).

Drucker, P.F. 1946. *Concept of the Corporation* (New York: John Day).

Drucker, P.F. 1951. *The New Society* (London: Heinemann).

Drucker, P.F. 1954. *The Practice of Management* (New York: Harper & Row).

Drucker, P.F. 1964. 1989. *Managing for Results* (London: Heinemann).

Drucker, P.F. 1966. 1967. *The Effective Executive* (New York: Harper & Row).

Drucker, P.F. 1969. *The Age of Discontinuity* (London: Heinemann).

Drucker, P.F. 1974. *Management: Tasks, Responsibilities, Practices* (London: Heinemann).

Drucker, Peter F. 1985. *Innovation and Entrepreneurship* (London: Heinemann).

Drucker, P.F. 1989, 1990. *The New Realities* (London: Heinemann Professional Publishing; Mandarin Paperback).

Drucker, P.F. 1992. *Managing for the Future – The 1990s and Beyond* (New York: Truman Talley Books).

Enriquez, J. 2003. *Gelecek Peşinizde* (Istanbul: Eczacıbasi).

Eslen, N. 2003. *Tarih Boyu Savaş ve Strateji* (Istanbul: Q-Matris).

Evans, P. and Wurster, T.S. 2000. *Blown to Bits: How the New Economics of Information Transforms Strategy* (Boston, MA: Harvard Business School Press).

Fayol, H., trans. Constance Storrs 1949. *General and Industrial Management* (London: Pitman).

Franklin, B. 1986. *The Way to Wealth* (Bedford: Applewood Books).

Fukuyama, F. 2004. *State Building: Governance and World Order in the Twenty-First Century* (Ithaca, NY: Cornell University Press).

Gelb, M.J. 1999. *Leonardo Da Vinci gibi Düşünmek* (Istanbul: Beyaz Yayinlari).

Güvenç, B. 2000. *Türk Kimliği: Kültür Tarihinin Kaynakları* (Istanbul: Remzi Kitabevi).

Hagstrom, R.G. Jr. 1994. *The Warr Buffett Way: Investment Strategies of the World's Greatest Investor* (New York: John Wiley).

Hamel, G. and Prahalad, C.K. 1994. *Competing for the Future: Breakthrough Strategies for Seizing Control of Your Industry and Creating the Markets of Tomorrow* (Boston, MA: Harvard Business School Press).

Handy, C. 1976. *Understanding Organizations* (Harmondsworth: Penguin).

Handy, C. 1984, 1986. *The Future of Work* (Oxford: Blackwell).

Handy, C. 1989, 1990. *The Age of Unreason* (London: Business Books).

Handy, C. 1990. *Inside Organizations: 21 Ideas for Managers* (London: BBC Books).

Handy, C. 1994. *The Empty Raincoat: Making Sense of the Future* (London: Random House).

Handy, C. 2001. *The Elephant and the Flea: Looking Backwards to the Future* (London: Random House).

Harmon, R.L. and Peterson, L.D. 1990. *Reinventing the Factory: Productivity Breakthroughs in Manufacturing Today* (New York: The Free Press).

Heilbroner, R.L. 1953. *The Worldly Philosophers: The Lives, Times and Ideas of Great Economic Thinkers* (New York: Simon & Schuster).

Henderson, B.D. 1984. *The Logic of Business Strategy* (Cambridge: Ballinger Publishing).

Herzberg, F. 1966. *Work and the Nature of Man* (New York: World Publishing).

Humble, J.W. 1971. *Management by Objectives* (Maidenhead: McGraw-Hill).

Jaques, E. 1976. *A General Theory of Bureaucracy* (London: Heinemann).

Juran, J.M. 1988. *Juran on Planning for Quality* (New York: Free Press).

Kanter, R.M. 1989. *When Giants Learn to Dance* (New York and London: Allen & Unwin).

Kennedy, P. 1987. *Economic Change and Military Conflict from 1500 to 2000: The Rise and Fall of the Great Powers* (New York: Random House).

Levitt, T. 1983. *The Marketing Imagination* (New York: McGraw-Hill).

Likert, R. 1961. *New Patterns of Management* (New York: McGraw-Hill).

Maslow, A.H. 1970. *Motivation and Personality* (New York: Harper & Row).

Mayo, E. 1949. *The Social Problems of an Industrial Civilization* (London: Routledge and Kegan Paul).

McGregor, D. 1960. *The Human Side of Enterprise* (New York: McGraw-Hill).

Miles, I. and Keenan, M. 2003. *Handbook of Knowledge Society Foresight* (Dublin: European Foundation for the Improvement of Living and Working Conditions).

Mintzberg, H. 1989. *Mintzberg in Management* (New York: Free Press).

Neave, H.R. 1990. *The Deming Dimension* (Knoxville, TN: SPC Press).

Ohmae, K. 1982, 1983. *The Mind of the Strategist* (New York: McGraw-Hill).

Ohmae, K. 1985. *Triad Power: the Coming Shape of Global Competition* (New York: Free Press).

Ohmae, K. 1990. *The Borderless World* (New York: Harper Business).

Özözer, Y. 2004 *Ne Parlak Fikir – Yaratıcı Düşünce Yöntemleri* (Istanbul: Sistem Yayincilik).

Paret, P. 1986. *Markers of Modern Strategy: from Machiavelli to the Nuclear Age* (Princeton, NJ: Princeton University Press).

Pascale, R.T. 1990. *Managing On the Edge* (New York: Simon & Schuster).

Peters T. 1987, 1988. *Thriving on Chaos* (New York: Alfred A. Knopf).

Peters T. and Austin, N. 1985. *A Passion for Excellence* (London: Collins).

Peters, T. and Waterman, R.H. Jr. 1982. *In Search of Excellence* (New York and London: Harper & Row).

Peterson, P.G. 1999. *How the Coming Age Wave Will Transform the World* (New York: Times Books, Random House).

Porter, M.E. 1980. *Competitive Strategy: Techniques for Analyzing Industries and Competitors* (New York: Free Press).

Porter, M.E. 1985. *Competitive Advantage* (New York: Free Press).

Porter, M.E. 1986. *Competition in Global Industries* (Cambridge, MA: Harvard Business School Press).

Porter, M.E. 1990. *The Competitive Advantage of Nations* (London: Macmillan).

Postrel, V. 2003. *The Substance of Style* (New York: HarperCollins).

Raiffa, H. 1982. *The Art and Science of Negotiation: How to Resolve Conflicts and Get the Best out of Bargaining.* (Cambridge, MA: Harvard University Press).

Revans, R.W. 1966. *The Theory of Practice in Management* (London: Macdonald).

Revans, R.W. 1971. *Developing Effective Managers* (New York: Praeger).

Saribay, A.Y. 2001. *Postmodernite, Sivil Toplum ve İslam* (Istanbul: Alfa Basim Yayim Dağitim).

Schonberger, R.J. 1986. *World Class Manufacturing* (New York: Free Press).

Schumacher, E.F. 1973. *Small is Beautiful* (London: Blond & Briggs).

Schwartz, P. 1991. *The Art of the Long View: Planning for the Future in an Uncertain World* (New York: Doubleday Dell).

Singer, C. 1959. *A History of Scientific Ideas: From the Dawn of Man to the Twentieth Century* (New York: Oxford University Press).

Slater, R. 1999. *Jack Welch and the Ge Way: Management Insights and Leadership Secrets of the Legendary CEO* (New York: McGraw-Hill).

Sloan, A.P. 1963, 1966, 1986. *My Years with General Motors* (New York: Doubleday).

Soros, G., 2004 *Açık Toplum, Küresel Kapitalizm'de Reform* (Istanbul: Truva Yayinlari).

Stern, C.W. and Stalk, G. Jr. 1998. *Perspectives on Strategy* (New York: John Wiley).

Taylor, F.W. 1947. *Scientific Management* (New York: Harper & Row).

Thorpe, S. 2000. *Einstein gibi Düşünmek* (Istanbul: Beyaz Yayınları).

Titiz, T.M. 2004. *Türkiye'de Devlet Denetiminde Reformlar ve Başarılarının Değerlendirilmesi* (Istanbul: TESEV).

Türkiye Ekonomik ve Toplumsal Tarih Vakfi 2002. *STK'larda Gönüllülük ve Gençlik* (Istanbul: Tarih Vakfi Yayınlari).

Türkiye Ekonomik ve Toplumsal Tarih Vakfi 2003. *Tarihin Kötüye Kullanımı* (Istanbul: Tarih Vakfi Yayınlari).

Tzu, S. 1983. *The Art of War* (New York: Bantam Doubleday Dell).

Usşak, C., Baldik, Ö. and Türkay, K. 2001. *Çoğulculuk ve Toplumsal Uzlaşma* (Istanbul: Abant Platformu Yayinlari).

Vasconcellos e sa, J. 1999. *The War Lords: Measuring Strategy and Tactics for Competitive Advantage in Business* (New Haven, CT: Kogan Page).

Von Weizsbackler, E., Lovins, A.B., Day, R., and Lovins, L.H. 1997. *Factor Four: Doubling Wealth, Halving Resource Use* (London: Earthscan Publications).

Waterman, R.H. Jr. 1987. *The Renewal Factor* (New York: Bantam).

Weber, M. 1930. *The Protestant Ethic and the Spirit of Capitalism* (London: Allen & Unwin).

Weber, M. 1947. *The Theory of Social and Economic Organization* (New York: Free Press).

Williamson, J. 1994. *The Political Economy of Policy Reform* (Washington, DC: Institute for International Economics).

Womack, J.P. and Jones, D.T. 1996. *Lean Thinking: Banish Waste and Create Wealth in Your Cooperation* (New York: Simon & Schuster).

Index